THE

NAZIR AFZAL

RACE

HOW TO FIGHT STRUCTURAL RACISM

TO THE

'THE AUTHENTIC FACE OF BRITISH JUSTICE'
THE NEW YORK TIMES

'CHAMPION OF THE IGNORED'
THE SUNDAY TIMES

TOP

Harper
North

HarperNorth
Windmill Green
24 Mount Street
Manchester M2 3NX

A division of
HarperCollins*Publishers*
1 London Bridge Street
London SE1 9GF

www.harpercollins.co.uk

HarperCollinsPublishers
Macken House
39/40 Mayor Street Upper
Dublin 1
D01 C9W8

First published by HarperNorth in 2022
This edition published by HarperNorth in 2023

1 3 5 7 9 10 8 6 4 2

A catalogue record for this book
is available from the British Library

HB ISBN: 978-0-00-848769-0
PB ISBN: 978-0-00-848772-0

Printed and bound in Great Britain by
CPI Group (UK) Ltd, Croydon

This book is produced from independently certified FSC™ paper
to ensure responsible forest management.

For more information visit: www.harpercollins.co.uk/green

To our parents, who paved the way

CONTENTS

METHODOLOGY

My approach to this book has been to reach out to senior leaders of colour in important sectors of British society to understand their experiences of racism, if any, while at or near the top of their professional journeys.

I invited them to share the challenges they face and to articulate any thoughts they may have on why they experienced what they did and how it can be mitigated for future generations who might aspire to follow the same path.

A large number were keen to talk about it on the record, in the main, though some asked that parts of their commentary be anonymised. A not insignificant group of others would only speak to me on condition of full anonymity and that no possible jigsaw identification would be possible.

This proved very challenging because, in many sectors and professions, the number of senior leaders of colour is so small that it would be possible to identify them or at the very least ensure that every one of these leaders – even those whom I had not spoken to – would fall under suspicion.

I routinely heard from these leaders that they believed their career profession would be further damaged if how they had been treated became known. The culture of fear that they consistently described was one I recognised and that was palpable, not paranoid. People who did not know each other, who worked in different fields and different parts of the country described the same fear.

Others had already been forced to sign non-disclosure agreements as part of internal settlements of their grievances. They painted a picture of institutions that wanted silence from them in order to protect organisational reputation. Individuals subject to these agreements were the most fearful because they not only expected their careers to be blighted but for legal consequences to follow if they spoke publicly.

I have reassured all contributors that their wishes will be respected. I will not be naming them and will guarantee anonymity to those who requested it.

Finally, all readers will be aware that language is continually evolving when talking about race and ethnicity. The UK civil service has recently scrapped the BAME label when referring to different ethnic minority groups. But in order to give interviewees the freedom to express themselves, I have chosen not to enforce any one-size-fits-all categorisation. So you will see different terminology throughout the book reflecting the conversations we had with the individuals concerned.

Nazir Afzal OBE

PROLOGUE

First they called me nigger. Then they called me Paki.

When *Love they Neighbour* was on TV in the 1970s, they called me Sambo.

The kinder ones would say, 'Oh look it's Sammy Davis Junior', after the only black face on TV who often wore glasses.

They said I 'smelt of curry', or lived in an Indian restaurant. I never did.

Dozens told me to go back to my country, but most of them could never decide what country or even continent that was. When I was a 'monkey', it was Africa.

I didn't have an accent. Not even a hint of Brummie burr from the city where I was born. But they would mimic some accent they'd overheard in a shop or from TV and pretend that was how I spoke. Politely, I would repeat myself even though I knew I had been understood, and they would mimic that accent again.

I was good at running but I had so much practice it shouldn't surprise you. A lot of my generation of children of immigrants spent much of our childhood sprinting from one potential attack to another. If a police officer saw you running away they would stop you and suspect you of shoplifting or some other offence, rather than take to task the boys chasing you. There was no hiding place, no sanctuary and no respite.

Back then my religion was a mystery to them, but imagine what they would have called me if Muslims were perceived as some are today.

I had a loving upbringing. But once I left the safety of home, I often felt hateful eyes boring into me. My crime was possessing an offensive face. There was nothing I could do about it but run.

When I share my formative experiences with people now, many assume it's 'ancient history', 'a rite of passage', or simply what happened 'back then'. Worse, when they know I became Chief Prosecutor and then the Chief Executive of Police Commissioners, the reaction is invariably, 'Well, look how far we've come, you're a shining example of how little racism there is now and how tolerant we are as a society.'

The problem is this isn't true. The past isn't a foreign country to me. In many ways they still do things the same now. Just in a more 'socially acceptable' way.

I have been hounded by racists all my professional life, had thugs outside my home, been thoroughly harassed both online and in the real world. I have had professional colleagues treat me differently simply because of how I look. And the highlights of my career have always been tainted by a racist response from some quarter or other.

My progress has been a battle when it should not have been, and sadly I'm not the only one. I have seen other people of colour being treated with prejudice and bigotry by people who claim to represent the more tolerant world we live in.

This matters because leadership is arguably the most powerful means of unlocking people's potential to become better.

As I write this, people of colour are still woefully under-represented in leadership positions across all sectors. Can it be acceptable in 2022 that there are no ethnic minority chief constables, no CEOs in the top 50 NHS Trusts and no permanent secretaries in the civil service?

Is it right that almost a quarter of the way into the twenty-first century, Britain has no ethnic minority Supreme Court Judges, no CEOs of the top financial institutions and only one union leader?

This lack of ethnic minority leaders doesn't just extend to public institutions either. Black employees, for example, hold just 1.5 per cent of top management roles in the UK private sector.

The fact that not one top civil servant, intelligence agency head, or top banking or media agency chief executive in Britain is from an ethnic minority speaks volumes.

But these statistics only tell half the story.

They don't tell us what stops people of colour getting the top jobs. And they don't reveal the hurdles used to prevent ethnic minority talent from progressing to the top. Nor do they speak of the journey of those who have managed to buck the trend. What can we learn from their experience that will enable us to roll back roadblocks to opportunity and ensure Britain benefits from more diverse leadership?

This book goes in search of these answers.

Not just because it seeks to understand why the diaspora of talent and drive that has so enriched modern Britain is all too often denied a seat at the top table. But mainly because it recognises that the progress a new generation demands has to be meaningful and not just a band-aid exercise.

There will be people who say Britain is a much more tolerant country than others and it is true that, globally, racism is on the rise. In the 2022 Edelman Trust Barometer, which surveyed people in 28 countries, it found that 57 per cent of respondents were worried about experiencing prejudice or racism. Across the world, divisions are widening and Britain is no exception.

The febrile mood that has accompanied the Black Lives Matter global movement is only likely to double down on a commitment for change. And it needs to be more than celebrities taking the knee, hashtags against racism, or black and ethnic minorities featuring on British coins and notes.

It needs to be *real* change.

If there's one thing I've learned, it's that the nature of injustice is such that we may not always see it. Throughout my career I've discovered that structural injustice can be hard to define, precisely because it's so ordinary. It's because things have always been a certain way that people often struggle to see how injustice is so deeply embedded in the fabric of our institutions.

As you will see over the following pages, the old boys' network is still very much alive and well. For change to happen we'll need to pull up some deep roots and break out of a back-scratching bubble. A Britain of all the talents won't come about simply because some politician says it will.

It will happen when cultural change makes it unacceptable to hold talent back and when progress is negotiated through moral courage by people doing what's right for everyone.

I hope you'll join with me to make it happen.

INTRODUCTION

In the summer of 2010 change was sweeping through Britain. We were in the early days of the first Coalition government since 1945, and as Clegg and Cameron put on an almost brotherly show of togetherness, there was a sense that the old political certainties were beginning to break up.

I felt this acutely in my work too, but some certainties remained unbreakable: notably people's ability to commit unspeakable crimes.

In June, a taxi driver named Derrick Bird left his home in Cumbria in the early hours and drove a few miles to a small hamlet on the western edge of the Lake District. Under the cover of darkness, he pulled up outside a house, entered his twin brother's home and shot him 11 times in the head and body with a .22 calibre rifle.

From there Bird went on a shooting spree that killed 12 people and injured 11 others before he eventually turned the gun on himself. One of his victims was a tourist, who Bird pulled up alongside in his car and asked if she was having a nice day. He then shot her in the face.

Bird's crimes would send shockwaves across the nation and generate a huge amount of media attention. And as is frequently the case with tragedy, some people used it to advance their own agendas. Three days later a man called Danny Lockwood wrote a column in *The Press*, a local newspaper in Dewsbury, West Yorkshire, arguing that Bird would have been celebrated by Muslim communities had he been carrying a copy of the Koran during his murderous campaign.

Naturally, this caused great offence and you can imagine the outcry among the local Muslim communities. Pressure was quickly applied on the police to take some action against Lockwood and it wasn't long before we had a decision to make on whether he could be prosecuted for inciting religious hatred.

The Crown Prosecution Service (CPS) applied the law to the facts and, after careful consideration, determined that it was not possible to prosecute him because the law required violence or threats of violence and Lockwood had done neither. We were satisfied this was the right decision but knew it was going to be extremely difficult to communicate. Lockwood subsequently apologised for what he had written.

At the time, the offended community had been protesting 24 hours a day outside Dewsbury police station and they couldn't understand why Lockwood hadn't been arrested. Several hundred protesters gathered and the police weren't sure how to communicate with them without inflaming tensions further. After reflecting upon the lack of diversity within their management team, senior police leaders realised they had nobody who could communicate to the protesters and win their trust.

The same applied to the local Council. The chief executive was fully aware of the complexities of the matter, but did not have anybody that they felt could sensitively and reassuringly communicate the decision. Ultimately, the decision was that of the CPS and it was down to us to communicate it. Of course, this could have been done by press release alone but everyone realised this wouldn't take the heat out of the situation.

Someone had to be found to go to Dewsbury to communicate the decision – and I was seen as the obvious choice.

At the time I was in a temporary role between being acting Chief Prosecutor in London and soon-to-be new Chief Prosecutor in northwest England. When I received the call to ask if I'd go and explain our decision, it was made very clear that I didn't have a choice. No other agency had anybody senior enough, black or Asian enough, or Muslim enough to provide a level of reassurance and stop a local problem becoming a flashpoint.

So the next day I found myself boarding a train at King's Cross and heading north to a part of the country I'd never been to before. When I walked into an annexe to the mosque in Dewsbury, the tension was palpable and hundreds of suspicious faces peered back at me.

I was flanked by a white police leader, a senior white Council Officer and a white prosecutor. The room was silent and they sat sipping water at a table while I stood up and made my way to the front.

'I know how hurtful Lockwood's comments were,' I began. 'They were as upsetting to me, as they are to you. I feel what you feel, but all I can do is apply the law of this country and, in this case, I have to demonstrate the threat of violence to prosecute.'

I paused for a moment, scanned the room and held my hands out in an open gesture

'I'm afraid there isn't the evidence to do that.'

Murmurs rippled through the room before someone spoke up.

'The problem is the law. Our politicians are letting us down!'

I had diffused a tense situation and they understood why the CPS had decided not to prosecute Lockwood. Afterwards, I shook hands and a number of people asked for a selfie.

All it needed was someone from within their own community to show empathy and explain in person how the CPS had come to its decision. Had anyone else on the panel said what I'd said, they wouldn't have been believed.

The problem here was that the communities that were offended, raw and tired of being abused, had no faith in the institutions that were meant to protect them. The leaders of these institutions did not reflect in any way the diversity of the community. A hostile and tense environment had to be neutralised and they had nobody to do it.

Diversity in this instance was not just about numbers or quotas, it was about being able to do your job effectively. The failures in institutional recruitment and promotion practices were laid bare and potentially could have sparked more unrest.

Looking back at this episode now, I'm reminded of just how important representation is for public bodies.

Diversity is not only essential to foster a better understanding and win hearts and minds. It's vital to building trust and maintaining social cohesion. And trust is the foundation upon which the legitimacy of public institutions is built. Without trust, support for reforms is hard to mobilise and policy-making becomes ever more difficult.

But a lack of diversity not only creates a lack of trust – it can also lead to worse health outcomes. A study in the *British Medical Journal*, for example, shows that doctors from underrepresented communities need to be present in increased numbers in leadership and decision-making roles, as data shows that patients have worse health outcomes when treated by physicians who do not have their shared experience.

'People are dying because of these unconscious or conscious biases against our patients,' argues Dr Shannon Ruzycki. 'I think we need to represent the population that we serve so we can start to improve health outcomes for our patients.'

It's not just public bodies that need to take the issue of diversity seriously, though. Business does, too, because without it their products or services will not represent the consumers they wish to serve.

Take the technology companies. When new technology is tested on small, unrepresentative groups of people, it can lead to chronic failure.

In artificial intelligence, an area of computer science that's become an integral part of our lives, we have seen voice recognition systems unable to understand ethnic minorities, AI algorithms prioritise the care of healthy white patients over sicker black patients, and Google's image-recognition algorithm has mistakenly tagged African Americans as 'gorillas' in the past.

Without diverse leadership in technology companies, racial bias is embedded in systems that we rely on in all sorts of areas, from law enforcement surveillance, passenger screening and employment, housing and credit decisions.

Studies have shown that millions of people have been affected by racial bias in healthcare algorithms. We've seen algorithmic risk assessments in courts disproportionately offer no bail release to white defendants instead of black defendants, and we've seen facial recognition technology misidentifying African and Asian faces.

The world's largest scientific computing society has called for a complete halt in the use of facial recognition technologies due to 'clear bias based on ethnic, racial, gender and other human characteristics'. What this means in practice is that people of colour are wrongly arrested as crime suspects after cameras scan their faces when they pass by in the street and match them with suspects from a watch list. One facial recognition tool, for example, wrongly flagged a university student as a suspect in the Sri Lankan bombings, who later went on to receive death threats.

All of this adds to a damning charge sheet. A failure to communicate, loss of trust, vital services being infected by racial biases, and essential technologies actively discriminating against significant swathes of the population.

The so-called culture wars may have reduced diversity to a tokenised buzzword or a lightning rod for frenzied, often factually challenged, attacks from all points of the political spectrum. But it should never be seen as an optional extra.

Diversity is needed to make the world fairer, get the most out of people's talent and allow organisations to meet the needs of the people they serve. And at a time when leaders are expected to navigate greater uncertainty and take charge of rapid change, we cannot possibly hope to lift capabilities by continuing to fall back on traditional models and mindsets.

Diversity needs to be at the heart of our post-Covid recovery and the modern Britain we aspire to be. Not a side agenda.

But, as argued in the coming pages, we won't make any real progress on fully breaking down barriers until we properly understand the scale of the problem.

1

THE CRIMINAL JUSTICE SYSTEM

Removing the blindfold and tipping the scales

Above the Central Criminal Court in England and Wales, commonly known as the Old Bailey, is a copper-roofed dome that's topped with an imposing 22-ton, 12-foot gold leaf statue of Lady Justice. Standing atop England's largest court house, she holds a sword in one hand and the scales of justice in the other, representing the swiftness and finality of justice and the weighing of the prosecution and defence. Modelled after the Roman goddess of justice, Iustitia, she cuts a dramatic figure against the rooftops and spires of London and has come to symbolise the ideal of law: even handedness, stability and equality.

However, there is one thing missing in this iconic representation.

Since the middle of the sixteenth century, the Roman goddess of justice has been pictured wearing a blindfold. It was introduced because of fears the justice system was tolerating abuse and influenced by politics, power and prejudice. The blindfold represented impartiality and objectivity, showing that justice should be meted out without fear or favour, regardless of wealth or your status in society.

It's an important omission. In courts around the world, Lady Justice wears a blindfold. But the Old Bailey courthouse brochures say they have stuck with the pre-sixteenth-century version where she was originally not blindfolded.

Whatever their reasons, it sends a powerful message. For all her awe inspiring majesty, justice is not blind.

Of course, many would argue that they don't need a statue to tell them this. After all, every year another report tells us the UK justice system is hampered by prejudice.

Research commissioned by the Sentencing Council has shown that black and ethnic minority offenders are far more likely to be sent to prison for drug offences than other defendants. And Ministry of Justice analysis, commissioned by the Lammy Review, showed that young black people are nine times more likely to be locked up in England and Wales than white people.

Justice is certainly not blind, and there is mounting evidence that it's biased against people of colour.

One of my last acts as Chief Prosecutor was to formally complain about a District Judge whose actions had been brought to my attention by one of my prosecutors. In a magistrates' court in Preston, a white defendant had appeared in custody facing an allegation against a Miss Patel, a victim of colour. The judge insisted on the case going ahead for trial immediately that afternoon (it hadn't been listed for trial) and demanded that the victim be told to come to court. When my prosecutor rightly pointed out it was unlikely that anyone could drop everything they are doing at zero notice, the judge argued otherwise.

'It won't be a problem,' he said. 'She won't be working anywhere important where she can't get the time off. She'll only be working in a shop or an off-licence.'

When the prosecutor asked the judge to clarify these incendiary remarks, he went even further.

'With a name like Patel, and her ethnic background, she won't be working anywhere important where she can't get the time off,' he argued. 'So that's what we'll do.'

As it happens, Miss Patel was a professional who didn't have a shop. But the judge clearly believed that if your name is Patel, then that's the most you could expect.

As a result of a complaint lodged by the CPS, the judge resigned as a District Judge. Following an inquiry it was also found that he could no longer sit in judgement in respect of his other responsibility as a first tier Immigration Judge.

Imagine, if you will, how his overtly racist attitude might have impacted his decisions involving a lot more Patels, Singhs or Khans, who appeared before him simply asking for the right to stay in this country.

Justice is most definitely not blind.

I am quite sure this judge wasn't the only one in the justice system to hold racist views, as I've heard similar comments from senior figures during my career. The only way to drag the judiciary into the twenty-first century is to ensure greater diversity on the benches. And this is another area where progress is torturously slow.

There were many moments that convinced me this book needed writing, but among the daily injustices and continual backtracking on promises that regularly gnawed away at me was a series of phone calls that made my blood run cold.

If there is one area of leadership that can make a critical impact on removing the racial disparity that blights our justice system, it's ethnic minority judges.

Before we get to judges – the number of BAME lawyers appointed as Queen's Counsel (a rank from which many of the senior judiciary are recruited) remains woefully low; there are still only a handful of BAME females in silk – fewer than 20 at the last count. Progress is slow but there is a real question as to whether the Bar is doing enough, both in progression and retention, particularly of women from BAME backgrounds. Childbirth and caring responsibilities leading to career breaks have been identified as major reasons why, first, they choose not to apply and, secondly, why they can't find meaningful work on their return. The Bar actively encourages pro-bono work to enable applicants to develop the competencies required for progression, that is, working for free, which is valuable in itself, but difficult to do when you have bills to pay.

Over the course of several weeks, following an article I contributed to in *The Times*, I began to realise what they were up against, as 20 judges, virtually all from minority backgrounds, approached me to complain about their treatment.

'We are finished,' sighed one, as he rattled through examples of bullying, harassment and generally unfair treatment at the hands of some of the most senior members of the judiciary. Others described how 'secret soundings' impacted on their ability to progress and how the 'old boys' club' continued to flourish in what was, outwardly, a more transparent process.

Why did they approach me? Because they felt I could get their concerns heard. Why did they not say anything themselves? Because they were, and are, scared to death of victimisation and repercussions.

'I was told that I couldn't deal with that case because I wasn't a safe pair of hands, so they gave it to the less experienced white guy,' was one comment that played over and over in my mind, following a conversation about the allocation of cases and assessment and promotion of judges.

A 2019 report by Lynne Townley and Kaly Kaul QC indicates that those from minority backgrounds and other under-represented groups are far more likely to be victims of bullying at the Bar. Under-reporting is a major issue because people 'fear for their careers and further victimisation'. Things are in fact so bad that the Bar Council have had to invest in a reporting app whereby victims of bullying and harassment can log incidents anonymously, although no formal action can obviously be taken against the perpetrator on an anonymous report.

One lawyer, on condition of anonymity, told me, 'Barely a week goes by without me having to deal with inappropriate behaviour or language, either from solicitors instructing me or from fellow barristers'. Another said, 'all the good (best paid work) just passes me by as if I'm not there. A new white male barrister with half my experience gets briefs [cases] that I just don't.'

At court, the situation is no less toxic and women, in particular, have to bear the brunt of crass behaviour. 'If I'm not told that I'm shaggable, I'm told I'm an ugly black bitch, there's no in between.' Why not report it, I ask, as these are strong capable advocates. 'It's career ending, not for the sexist or racist, but for me,' I was told. Another was even more scathing. 'It's bad enough that your senior colleagues won't support you, but the people who run the system, they won't even do more than pay lip service.'

The words could have come straight from my mouth given the number of times it happened to me, but they were delivered by a judge and the 'they' it referred to were the senior judiciary of England and Wales.

We have truly come to a sorry pass when the people who sit in judgement on the rest of us are unable to talk about their own situation.

In 2020, there was just 1 ethnic minority Court of Appeal Judge and 4 High Court Judges. There were 27 Circuit Judges and, in total, they represented 8 per cent of all Court Judges. The judiciary is struggling to represent the people they serve and lags behind many other sectors. The 4 per cent of High Court Judges that are a minority compares to 10 per cent of MPs and 40 per cent of NHS consultants.

'The judiciary is 20 years behind the Metropolitan Police in accepting that it is institutionally racist,' was the damning accusation from an experienced judge of colour. This is even more shocking when you see the criticism being levelled at police in the light of recent events. 'The most senior judiciary use the independence of justice to hide this culture of racism, bullying and isolation,' another judge told me.

District Judge Claire Gilham won a seven-year fight against the Ministry of Justice as a whistleblower, after being sacked for revealing racism and bullying by some of her colleagues. She says, 'The justice system says there is no bullying, there is no racism. It actually destroys its records and doesn't do proper investigations.' Another retired part-time judge who also fought successfully against the Ministry is Peter Herbert, a former Chair of the Black Society of Lawyers. He says, 'When the judiciary is faced with allegations that there is a lack of diversity, they refuse to adopt meaningful targets and then blame the Bar and Law Society for the racism which is within.'

In the 2020 Judicial Attitudes Survey, not one mention is made of bullying or racism. 'If it had asked specific questions,' said one judge of colour, 'they would have perhaps realised how disenchanted we are. They simply don't want to know and they're operating a "don't ask, don't tell" policy.' Another judge said, 'At private dinner parties, other judges will openly use racist remarks, so imagine what they do when we're not there.'

Following my public interventions, supported by bold national media and a couple of judges who had settled their individual legal actions, the Lord Chief Justice (the most senior criminal judge) announced a number of measures including a 'whistleblowing' process and additional training. Suffice to say, the judges who approached me were not impressed and had little confidence that it would make any real difference.

What they argue is that for too long the Judicial Office and Ministry of Justice have turned a blind eye to bullying, sexism and racism. They also wanted me to highlight the secrecy of judicial appointments and the 'black-balling' of judges who are not seen to toe the establishment line.

Judges complain that when they voice concerns they are ignored (ghosted), made to feel there is no problem (gaslit) or threatened or victimised.

This allows those with their hands on the levers of power to create a culture of fear and keep the status quo. In doing so, judges in all arenas are unable to dispense proper justice for fear of being reprimanded. That means the very people seeking justice have little or no protection. The bottom line is justice is not being served.

At the time of writing, in the past 18 months not one single person of colour has been appointed to the High Court bench or made a senior circuit judge. The Judicial Appointments Commission (JAC) refused a Freedom of Information request asking for the figures and process on the basis that this information would be published in the generic statistics. These statistics do not provide details of specific selection exercises, so judges feel aggrieved that they will not know how many people of colour applied for positions and how many were appointed.

Their concern is that after 15 years since the JAC was created under the terms of the Constitutional Reform Act of 2005, why does the judiciary not represent the wider society it serves? The judges I spoke to argue that the senior judiciary controls every aspect of the process and appointments, and it will only permit appointments in its own image.

Our justice system has a proud history and has influenced many jurisdictions. It used to be an article of faith that British justice is the finest in the world. However, that boast can no longer be made with the same confidence, as people are more likely to assert that British justice *used* to be the best in the world. As the conversations I've had painfully illustrate, even our own judges believe it's no longer pre-eminent.

Unfortunately, not nearly enough is known by the public of the prejudiced attitudes at the heart of our judiciary, as the spotlight invariably falls on frontline policing. Here, there is less ambiguity as a series of shocking exposés, particularly in relation to the Metropolitan Police, have shown racist attitudes among police to be a significant problem. In February 2022, the Independent Office for Police Conduct published a series of messages from WhatsApp groups and Facebook chats showing the scale of the problem.

'My dad kidnapped some African children and used them to make dogfood' is an example of the toxic nature of the messages.

I spoke to many current and former police officers about the challenges of making the police service more diverse and they all acknowledged that a better culture needed to be in place.

One former Superintendent, who I've afforded anonymity because of his fear of reprisals, spoke candidly about the dangerous groupthink in his force.

He joined the police in the 1980s and would become the most senior person of colour in his force. In his early days he vividly remembers hearing racist language but says the Macpherson Report in the wake of Stephen Lawrence's murder in 1993, which concluded that the Metropolitan Police were institutionally racist, forced racism underground.

'Before, I knew who the racists were. But after Macpherson you weren't sure,' he says. 'They knew they'd be sacked if they were openly racist.'

Despite being very capable and working harder than most, he recalls finding it difficult to get promoted and says he was never 'in the club'. Although he was eventually promoted to Superintendent, he was initially rejected after a hard-hitting conversation with senior officers.

'Look, you have to understand that they don't value talent or ability – they value loyalty and they want you to be just like them,' he explains. 'I was told that I wear their colours, their jacket and

I had to give total loyalty. "Will you lie, die or kill for us?" they demanded. I said I wouldn't do anything that wasn't right or just and that was the end of my application.'

He was, some years later, eventually recommended for promotion but said he was always seen as an outsider. 'Only one other superintendent came to my leaving-do when I retired.'

Even now he says there's a sense of distrust and suspicion towards people of colour in the force, as though they can't be relied on to toe the line.

'Just look at the news whenever the police are in the spotlight and being criticised,' he argues. 'Which former officer of colour anywhere in the UK will go on television and support the police? No one.'

This conversation played on my mind and a few weeks later I found myself talking to Lord Carlile QC about policing and diversity. As the son of Polish Jewish immigrants, he's a big believer that Britain has built its success based on talents from all races, religions and beliefs.

Right from the beginning of our discussion, he argued that there was limited diversity in policing and that continued evidence of racism in major forces like the Met provided a clear case study for newly proactive diversity across policing.

The problem as he saw it was that the police establishment 'is far too fragmented and clumsy to enable valued diversity policy to develop'.

Change, he argued, would not happen without major police restructuring.

'There are still 43 territorial police forces, some of which are quite small and have limited Human Resources capacity,' he explains. 'The argument for uniting some of these police forces, perhaps to create 10 territorial police services in England and Wales, is strong and would provide many benefits including improved diversity; but change is obstructed by the reluctance of ministers and local MPs to recognise the need for change to establish stronger forces with greater and wider capacity, capable of running successful diversity policies.'

With a 2021 HM Inspectorate of Constabulary in Scotland report showing that recruitment of females and people of ethnic minority backgrounds had increased over the last year, he added that this model could be a blueprint for more inclusive policing.

'In Scotland, despite some serious teething troubles, the establishment of a single force, Police Scotland, is now seen by officers and the wider world as more fair and diverse in its promotion policies than its fragmented predecessors.'

But whether solutions lie in better structures, more transparency or stronger, more capable leadership, the bottom line is always the same. Unless our justice systems embrace diversity, they will continue to have an inherent unfairness at their heart and let many communities down.

Fairness and rule of law are, after all, the basis of every person's rights in the UK. They are the cornerstones of a civilised society. They affect all of us. Rent increases, repossessions of homes, rights to health care for a disabled child, fathers' access rights, debts, rights to bail and tax rebates are just some examples.

These are daily issues which matter to each and every person in the UK. The law is not abstract; it's inextricably bound up in our everyday lives, from birth certificates and names of children to a partner's right to a family home after separation, inheritance under wills, divorce arrangements, and the purchase of your own home. Everybody has to go through many legal processes in their life. Do you want people to have to *like* you to determine the rights and wrongs of such matters? Until the law is genuinely blind and doesn't discriminate, then rights have been replaced by a wicked game of chance.

I spoke to many lawyers in researching this book and because of its sensitive subject matter frequently got the same response. When

I asked lawyers about racism, they invariably were happy to talk about how bad it was but were afraid to put their own experiences on the record, because, as one put it, 'there will be consequences'.

One of the most troubling findings from these conversations was the weary resignation with which they had come to accept this bias. Indeed, many had priced it in to their career and had to creatively counter it in order to get ahead.

There is a growing controversy about what 'should' a lawyer look like? How far have we really come with diversity in the legal profession? Well, not very far if we look at the debate about court dress, particularly wigs – and whether they are culturally insensitive. Court wigs date back centuries and became formal court dress in 1685. They are no longer required in family or civil courts, but maintained in criminal cases. Leslie Thomas QC believes that the wig 'represents and signifies the culturally insensitive climate'. His comments followed a black barrister with an Afro, Michael Etienne, being told he faced disciplinary action if he did not wear his wig in court. When Mr Etienne wrote to the Bar Council to seek clarity, he was told that he could be held in contempt of court, face paying wasted costs of the hearing, and face 'various potential breaches of the Code of Conduct'. Barristers can apply for special dispensation if they don't want to wear a wig, including those who wear a turban or hijab, but as one said, 'The perception is that we are the strange ones.'

So, I heard stories of lawyers who changed their names to more English sounding ones in order to get job interviews. A Nigerian lawyer called Karibo, for example, became Kevin.

Then there was the large number of law firms run mostly by people of colour which have Anglo-Saxon names. Everyone I asked said the same thing. 'If we used our own names, it would put clients off and other lawyers would not take us seriously.' I had seen this myself when a judge turned his nose up at a firm with an obviously Asian sounding name. He repeated it three times for no reason, something he didn't do for Smith & Jones. The fact that lawyers at the top of their profession believe they have to hide behind an Anglo-Saxon name to get some credibility is shocking, but ultimately not surprising.

'The way we are treated by the Courts, by clients, by other lawyers and even by the Solicitor's Regulatory Authority (SRA) is bad enough when they know what our name is. Why should we make it worse by plastering our real names on our letterheads?' one solicitor explained to me.

The SRA is a case in point. They are meant to inspect and investigate allegations of wrong-doing by solicitors' firms, but tend to focus too much on firms containing people of colour. So much so that they have had to respond publicly to the criticism. In 2014, a report by Professor Gus John found black and Asian solicitors were disproportionately targeted for conduct investigations and called for the SRA to publish monitoring data on how its policies affected BAME solicitors.

More than five years later when public pressure saw the SRA finally publish figures, after they had previously told the Law Gazette that 'the balance of public interest' was in favour of withholding these figures, the numbers were almost identical to the treatment Professor John had discovered in 2014. It found that the number of people brought through disciplinary processes was disproportionately based on race: 31 per cent of those struck off were from an ethnic minority.

Now there might be good reason to investigate any firms containing people of colour. It's just unlikely that a disproportionate amount of bad practice can be found where a Patel, Singh or Khan works.

The President of the Law Society, I. Stephanie Boyce is the first black woman to hold this eminent position in its history. She, too, accepts that there has been disproportionate regulatory action against people from minority backgrounds because they are more likely to be in small firms. But that can't be the only reason, as the SRA has commissioned some research into disparities. When I spoke to her, she readily acknowledged that judicial diversity is a long way off and has made several calls for action requiring a shared ambition and commitment. However, she argued that white allies needed to pledge more support and own the issue as much as those from minorities. She still sees people being invited to join equality and diversity committees simply because they are black.

'I often hear the response to, "Where are your senior black staff?" is, "We have one on our diversity committee."'

Her own journey is described as challenging. She's clearly heard people say to her, 'Who does she think she is?' when conversations about her take place. She's learnt not to read comments online in order to protect her mental health.

In the course of our conversation, Boyce also conceded that if you're born a certain colour you can expect discrimination as more doors are shut, and therefore you need more determination. She learnt the hard way that you cannot please everyone, and micro-aggressions, commonplace daily verbal or behavioural indignities that communicate hostile or derogatory slights towards marginal groups are frequently overlooked – despite their negative impacts.

'I don't think the racism I have experienced is of the blatant kind, it's the subtle but no less pernicious variety,' she explains.

She recently moved into the Buckinghamshire countryside and her parents were anxious about the fact that she was pretty much the only non-white person in a population of about a thousand people. On one occasion somebody was looking at a new house nearby and she recalls how they were looking at her more than they needed to. Growing up she doesn't recall much racism in leafy England, she just calls it name-calling, but Covid has reminded her that other signs were there. People walking around each other socially distanced has reminded her of what it was like when she was growing up. Her father was bright but nobody wanted to take instructions from a black man so he had to work in a relatively low-skilled job. She also noticed people giving her family more space than they needed when they moved around.

She has regularly been asked, 'Where did you come from?' And told 'you're very articulate' as though she doesn't speak English as a first language. She recalls when she was overseeing an award ceremony at Law Society HQ, which she was conducting, how in the reception beforehand, despite everybody being dressed in black suits, that her offering her hand to families who had attended would often find her hand left hovering in mid-air until she told them who she was. Who did they think she was?

There are countless statistics, audits and reports showing unfairness at the heart of our justice system and a chronic lack of diversity in our senior judiciary. It could be argued that they are so prevalent that we have reached a point where many, including Theresa May's Race Disparity Audit, simply repeat what we already know. What follows is usually a collective hand wringing, mutterings about lessons needing to be learned and lip service commitments to do better.

But putting in place the building blocks of effective change leadership is continually overlooked.

However many well-intentioned nods to a more diverse and fairer judicial system there are, without new leadership there will be no change.

How then do those people of colour in the judiciary who hold leadership positions measure up? Do we have the right leaders to drive through change? That, I couldn't be sure of.

I've known Tan Ikram for two decades from when he was a solicitor appearing in magistrates' courts in Thames Valley, fighting for his clients, who were predominantly from minority backgrounds. Today he is the second most senior District Judge in the land, and deservedly so. I reminded him of the many conversations we had where we shared experiences of racist micro-aggressions and how he had felt that the Courts, the police and others had discriminated against his clients. Now, our conversation was entirely given over to the supposedly 'excellent initiatives driven by the judiciary and the professions' that have levelled the playing field.

'You'd struggle to find a white solicitor or barrister in some magistrates' courts,' he says. I ask him if the massive cuts in criminal legal aid might have meant that the white solicitors and barristers had stopped doing criminal casework and he shrugged, unable to answer.

I ask him if the research that indicates a black man is nine times more likely to be stopped and searched, more likely to be arrested, more likely to be charged, more likely to be convicted and more likely to be sentenced to prison – on exactly the same evidence as a white man – might suggest that the system remains institutionally racist? Again, he didn't know.

He was, however, at pains to express how 'committed the judiciary is to tackling hate crime and racism in particular', and on that we agree. However, he admitted that racism within the system is a 'work in progress'.

Dame Bobbie Cheema-Grubb, erstwhile High Court Judge, is a barrister I have admired for what seems like forever. She advocated in several of my most high-profile and often highly charged cases. The honour killing of Banaz Mahmod being one of them, which was recently turned into an ITV television drama called *Honour*, while I merely acted as a consultant for the producers.

I recall how she emailed me 15 years ago saying she wanted to be more involved in preventative work on honour crimes and asked me to introduce her to some non-governmental organisations (NGOs). This was an example of the dedication to justice which she has always been known for.

My attempts to interview her failed as I was told, 'High Court Judges don't do interviews.' But I know that she is working behind the scenes to diversify the profession in her role as a 'diversity champion'. Why, though, do only the black and brown judges become 'diversity champions'? Why can't they talk about what they're doing?

This lack of transparency feeds the narrative that not a lot has changed or is changing. The burden of change is falling on leaders of colour themselves.

The things that could make the biggest difference have long been known but, then again, maybe those in power don't want to make the biggest difference.

Targets for selection of judges have existed, but have no teeth and therefore there are no consequences if they're not met. So why not properly set them and make it a requirement that the senior judiciary explain to us through a parliamentary select committee if they're not met?

Similarly, we need to create a Judicial Career Path with all the appropriate tools and support in place so you can start as a Deputy District Judge or tribunal member and know how you can become a High Court Judge, rather than the papal white smoke approach that currently exists.

We also need active talent management which will fast stream the most capable, not just those whose mums and dads were judges.

There is space at the top, but progress is slow and, as we have seen, those that do rise will often encounter bullying and racism. It's not good enough to say, as one senior judge told me, 'They need to be resilient, they need to be strong, they need to overcome these obstacles'. They shouldn't have obstacles that relate to the colour of their skin and it's time they were cleared out of the way.

2

SPORTS

Seeing the invisible, doing the impossible

In any given year, there's always a sense of excitement at the start of Wimbledon when the top seeds are threatened with an early exit at the hands of up and coming talent. But as the oldest Grand Slam returned in 2021 after being cancelled the previous year for the first time since World War II, the atmosphere seemed more charged than usual.

In the first round, two matches stood out as potential banana skins for the pre-tournament favourites. On Centre Court, the world number one and reigning champion, Novak Djokovic, faced Jack Draper, a teenager billed as the best British hope since Andy Murray.

While on the other main showcourt, the third seed and French Open runner-up, Stefano Tsitsipas, faced the unseeded 23-year-old American Frances Tiafoe.

In many ways these matches perfectly encapsulated a problem that dogs elite sport in Britain; and they also captured what's most inspiring about tennis – and what's wrong with it.

On Centre Court, world number 253 Draper shot out of the blocks to win the first set and raise the prospect of a massive upset. Hitting crisp groundstrokes and landing unreturnable serves, it's easy to see why he's the subject of considerable hype. The high society publication *Tatler* is among those noting that the wildcard from Surrey 'has a dazzling future ahead'.

Draper is certainly a bright prospect, but as a private-school educated, son of former head of the Lawn Tennis Association (LTA) Roger Draper, his rise does little to help shake off the white elitist tag tennis suffers from in Britain – and it reinforces the view that it's not an inclusive sport, but draws from a narrow and privileged talent pool.

In the end, Draper's threat quickly fizzled out and Djokovic ran out a comfortable winner. But it did introduce Draper to living rooms around Britain and raise questions about the talent pipeline in British tennis. Why, for example, in recent years has over a quarter of a billion pounds of public investment to foster new talent in the men's game only produced (at the time of writing) one male Briton under 23 inside the Association of Tennis Professionals' top 300, who happens to be the son of the man who was in charge of tennis in Britain?

We will return to Draper's privilege shortly, but a far more inspiring contest was taking place at the same time on Court Number One.

There, Frances Tiafoe was playing the game of his life and using his unorthodox buggy-whip forehand to cause one of the shocks of the tournament by beating Tsitsipas, the highly rated Greek talent who had knocked Rafael Nadal out of the Australian Open earlier in the year.

Watching Tiafoe's style is equally fascinating and bewildering. His forehand employs an exaggerated swing to generate extra torque as his body turns through the ball to hit hard, heavy spinning groundstrokes. It's the antithesis to the natural elegance of someone like Roger Federer and is so awkward it looks like it shouldn't work.

But if he doesn't come across as a naturally graceful athlete and is instead more of a dynamic blur of aggressive perseverance, there's a good reason for it.

From an early age, Tiafoe taught himself to play tennis.

His upbringing couldn't have been more different to that of Jack Draper, who grew up in Wimbledon village and trained at a National Tennis Centre that his father had commissioned.

While Draper's journey to Wimbledon's hallowed lawns was aided by his dad's £650,000 salary (and lavish bonuses) as well as LTA funding and his pick of the best coaches and facilities in the country, Tiafoe's journey stands in stark contrast.

His family were born in the war-torn country of Sierra Leone, which has one of the worst life expectancy rates in the world. In 1996, the conflict was so bad his mother was going to a funeral every week. Desperate to flee the civil war, she was one of millions to enter the United States green card lottery, which randomly allocates 55,000 visas to people from countries with low immigration rates to the United States. The odds were unbelievably slim, but Tiafoe's parents struck lucky, were offered a visa and could choose a new life.

In America, his mother gave birth to twin brothers, and his father secured a job on a construction crew building a multi-court tennis facility in Maryland.

He threw himself into his work and did such a good job that the centre's owners offered him a job there as a janitor. To make more money he worked longer hours and eventually converted a storage room next to the coach's office into a living space. Both parents were working flat out to get by, and with his wife living in a one-bedroom flat and working night shifts as a nurse, his employer turned a blind eye and let his two young sons sleep there during the week.

This was how young Tiafoe was introduced to tennis. He and his brother would sleep on the floor and on massage tables, then, whenever he got the chance, Frances would head to the practice courts and spend hours on end watching people playing tennis. His first memory as a toddler was of his father holding his hand while he hit a ball against a backboard.

As a 6-year-old, Frances would wander the grounds of the complex and watch the coaches put older players through their paces. He was like litmus paper, absorbing everything. Then he'd take his racket and go to the back wall of the facility and practise everything he'd seen.

By the time he was 12 Frances knew he wanted to be a professional tennis player.

His talent was immediately obvious but in a white, rich environment where senators' kids turned up in chauffeur-driven cars sporting the best designer gear, he stuck out like a sore thumb.

Other kids would mock him for the clothes he was wearing, laughing at the Pokémon Pikachu T-shirt he wore all the time on court. Others would tease him for the holes in his shoes.

The jibes hurt young Tiafoe but when he complained to his parents about it, his dad decided it was time he learned an important lesson.

Knowing his wife was going to a wedding in Freetown, he told her to take the boys along with her so they could compare their lives to the struggle of people in Sierra Leone.

It was a life-changing experience and years later Tiafoe would tell journalists how the grinding poverty he witnessed there jolted him to his senses, and made him realise how lucky he was.

'It humbled me and made me serious,' he told the BBC. 'It came into my head pretty quick to use tennis as a way to help not only myself, but our family because they have sacrificed so much.'

He's now one of the top-ranked American tennis players, has reached a Grand Slam quarter final, and has spoken about wanting to do for men's tennis what the Williams sisters did for women's tennis. Representation, he argues, is everything.

'That's what it's about,' he explained in an interview with Sky. 'It's not about hitting this tennis ball. It's putting guys in situations to be able to win, that's what I want to do with my platform . . . How do we make it a cool thing to get kids into it and teach them that it's not, so to speak, a white sport? That's the challenge.'

It certainly is – and while the US system is not perfect by a long stretch, it's hard to envisage a tennis player in Britain making the same journey as Tiafoe's.

America has a history of black tennis dating back to Althea Gibson and Arthur Ashe. Britain doesn't. It's a phenomenally white sport where people of colour are unlikely to see themselves represented. In the 2020 US Open, for example, there were 12 black American players in the women's draw. Only Heather Watson, whose mother is from Papua New Guinea, represented any kind of racial diversity among the British players.

Undoubtedly, this is a problem that's been caused by weak leadership at the LTA. For some time now they have been under pressure to move with the times and break out of an elitist and inward looking groupthink. MPs and Britain's most decorated player Andy Murray have criticised the fact that none of the 12 people on the All England Club Board and the 12 on the LTA board are from a BAME background.

However, it does appear that, finally, the penny is dropping. An LTA Inclusion Strategy was hurriedly rushed out in 2021 and the appointment of Sanjay Bhandari and Anil Jhingan as non-executive directors has at least started the process of reversing a terribly outdated old boys' club culture that has held the sport back for too long.

But while they are at last making an effort to join the twenty-first century, the LTA has a history of making pledges to embrace progress only to remain pickled in aspic. Few seem to have confidence that winds of change are sweeping through the sport.

'Tennis is an elitist sport. The majority of people involved are white and the majority are white men,' admits Miles Daley, a black tennis coach from Hackney, who is a member of the LTA's IDEA group, a diversity initiative aimed at opening up the sport.

'Tennis needs voices that are not saying "everything is OK". Because everything isn't OK,' he adds.

It certainly isn't, as many will testify.

Leading ethnic minority British tennis players such as Jay Clarke and Heather Watson have spoken of receiving so much racist abuse that it's become normalised. The number six ranked British player Clarke says he's racially abused 'at least once a day, nine days out of ten', while British number four, Heather Watson, said she'd received a handful of death threats and 'been called a monkey and told to go back to the zoo'.

It is, like a number of other sports in the UK, seen as inaccessible to large swathes of the population, notably people of colour. There are many reasons for this, but the main one, which is supported by research from the Sport and Recreation Alliance, is that too many sports clubs are not prepared to welcome ethnic minorities.

The research shows that 40 per cent of BAME participants say they have endured negative experiences in sport and physical activity settings, compared to only 14 per cent of white participants. These negative experiences relate to interaction with volunteers, coaches, staff at reception centres and online support.

For all the high-profile examples of racism at elite level in sport – from allegations of racist abuse towards youth team players at Chelsea and Newcastle, and the appalling culture of racism at Yorkshire County Cricket Club – there is little public awareness of the casual racism lower down the sporting chain, at grassroots level.

The delays to membership being processed, lack of game time, continual benching and being shunned on the courts by other members are just some of the experiences that were fed back to us when researching this book.

'Whenever I'd turn up to a club night, every excuse was made so I couldn't play,' one person said of their experience at a local tennis club. 'I'd be told there was no one to play with me at the moment and to wait until someone else turned up later. But no one did and I was made to feel really unwelcome.'

'As soon as I stepped on to the pitch,' another said of his experience at a football club, 'it was obvious I wasn't welcome. No one passed the ball to me and, whenever I got a touch, others would immediately try to foul me. I left at half time and no one said anything.'

'I thought I'd try a club night and was shunned by other players,' another said of their tennis experience. 'When I hit a few loose shots, someone asked if I'd ever thought of playing basketball instead.'

A common theme that runs through too many overwhelmingly white sports – whether it's tennis, golf, rowing, swimming or cricket – is that many people of colour are made to feel this is not *their* sport and they don't belong.

The latter example of cricket, which is a sport that's considered to be England's national game and was invented in this country, is arguably the most egregious.

Despite having one of the highest participation rates among British south Asians, this is a sport where barriers to people of colour making it professionally have been in place for decades.

Thanks to the Yorkshire all-rounder, Azeem Rafiq, awareness of an unforgiving and ugly culture of racism at the heart of Yorkshire cricket is now burned into the public's consciousness. But it has deeper roots than most people imagine.

If 2021 was the year that England finally faced up to the fact that their national sport, a game they exported to the world, was so mired in prejudice that its most historically successful club conceded it was institutionally racist, then it does beg the question: why has this time of reckoning taken so long?

For as long as I can remember, racism has been commonplace in cricket. You couldn't miss it when the England captain Tony Greig promised to make the West Indies team 'grovel'. It was there again in Norman Tebbit's cricket test to measure the loyalty of immigrants. And you could also see it in Ian Botham's crass remark that 'Pakistan is the kind of place that you send your mother-in-law for a month'. It was everywhere. In interviews, political speeches and, more menacingly, in far-right threats like those that black all-rounder Phillip DeFreitas received from the National Front when he was warned, if he played for England, he would be shot.

No matter how hard you tried to pretend racism in cricket wasn't a problem, it always slid back into view like shark fins rising from seemingly calm waters.

Long before Azeem Rafiq painfully described a culture where fans threw a pig's head at Pakistan supporters and poured beer over a young Muslim child, while players made the dressing room a cauldron of racist hatred, there were plenty of other warnings that should have been heeded.

Over 20 years ago, the *Wisden Cricketers' Almanack*, known as the bible of cricket, warned that 'cricketing apartheid' had become 'accepted practice' in England. 'There is now clear cut evidence of segregation operating, informally, in both Yorkshire and Essex,' the editor wrote in the editorial to the 1999 edition. In the same year Imran Khan, widely considered as one of the game's greatest all-rounders, who went on to become Prime Minister of Pakistan, warned that Asian players in England had complained about racism for many years.

'With Yorkshire, which is flooded with Asian people, how come an Asian just doesn't find a place?' he asked while commentating at the Cricket World Cup final. 'It baffles me. There's got to be an element of some prejudice.'

Nowadays, there's no need for such conjecture. When Ebony Rainford-Brent, the first black woman to play cricket for England, warned that the sport 'structurally has a lot of problems that doesn't allow diversity to come through from the local communities', she highlighted how cricket systematically locks out talent.

As Director of Women's Cricket at Surrey, she could see irrefutable evidence of this on her doorstep. In the local Borough of Lambeth, for example, where 'almost 50 per cent of the kids are from an African-Caribbean background', she has criticised the lack of opportunity, noting how in the last 25 years, 'we have not had one story successfully staying in county cricket since I've come through that door'.

This absence of opportunity can be seen right across the country. The fact that around 30 per cent of grassroots cricket players are of south Asian heritage, while only 4 per cent of British professionals are British south Asian shows how much potential is going to waste. This elitist approach is further evidenced by a study from the social mobility charity, the Sutton Trust, which showed that 43 per cent of men and 35 per cent of women playing cricket for England came from private schools. When you consider only 7 per cent of the country attend private schools, it shows a sport that's dripping with privilege. Such a narrow, elitist focus not only harks back to the nineteenth century, but makes a mockery of the millions invested by Sport England to support the next generation of talented cricketers and widen participation.

As with tennis, there are countless initiatives which claim to be widening cricket, but all the evidence shows it is failing and remains a sport riddled with nepotism, class and elitist groupthink. The England and Wales Cricket Board's 'Inspiring Generations' strategy document for 2020–2024 laughably claims to connect communities to the game and ensure cricket 'belongs to us all'.

Scyld Berry, the former editor of *Wisden*, is someone who knows the difference between the reality at the grassroots and well-meaning but ultimately meaningless rhetoric about the game belonging to everyone. He's already warned that cricket is in danger of becoming a sport of 'a privileged and receding niche' and provides a fair few hard hitting statistics to prove it.

Arguably the most chilling one is the fact that 25 per cent of England test cricketers have had a brother, father or uncle who played for the team. This is a damning indictment of a rigged system based on privilege that's light years away from being meritocratic.

This old boys' network has deep roots in the sport and it is incredible that it's taken the courage of Azeem Rafiq in speaking out against systemic discrimination across the game to finally shine an unforgiving light on it.

When I sit down with Rafiq to discuss what he's been through, the first thing that strikes me is that he appears exhausted. He looks like a man carrying the world on his shoulders.

Of course, in many respects he is. He's the first to admit that, 'when I spoke out, I spoke as a broken man that had just had enough'. Since then he's been at the centre of a media storm, appeared before MPs in Parliament, been subject to intense scrutiny and hailed by thousands for his bravery in speaking out.

It's an act that cost him his career as a cricketer. His mental health suffered badly and he contemplated suicide. But, despite the obvious pain you can see etched on his face, he retains an enormous passion for the game, which is matched by his determination to bring about lasting change.

Rafiq came to the UK as a 9-year-old and would captain the England under-15 side before making his senior debut for Yorkshire at 17. There's pride in his voice, which is distinctively Yorkshire, as he reflects on his achievements. But he also talks about his sadness at the talent that's going to waste all over the country, as 'amazing Asian players' are not getting the chances they deserve. He says there are hardly any non-white coaches in England and a dominant mindset that has no appetite to make the game more diverse. And current cricketing structures are almost guaranteed to make sure this remains.

'How can it be that if you are white and privately educated you have 33 times more chance of playing professional cricket?' he asks, quoting recent PhD research.

Rafiq's incredibly raw and painful testimony, which included inhuman treatment by Yorkshire County Cricket Club after his unborn child died, has been branded cricket's 'Me Too' moment. Yet, while this has ensured a powerful spotlight has finally fallen on cricket, with the England and Wales Cricket Board charging Yorkshire and several individuals with bringing the game into disrepute, he is unconvinced it's bringing the change that's needed.

'There are 18 [cricketing] counties and 17 counties don't see this as a problem,' he says, noting the 'hurtful stereotypes' used by the chairman of Middlesex, Mike O'Farrell when he spoke before a digital, culture, media and sport select committee.

Incredibly, O'Farrell told MPs that the south Asian community didn't have the commitment to play professional cricket because 'they prefer to go into other educational fields'.

It was a clumsy, racist and untrue assertion that's wildly at odds with the enormous passion and love of the game shown by south Asians in Britain.

When I ask Rafiq about his own childhood and the origins of his love for the game, he smiles and his face lights up.

'I grew up in Pakistan and it's religion there,' he says. 'I started watching cricket on television with my grandad and that's where it started. As soon as I could walk, I was playing on the streets of Karachi for six or seven hours after school.

'I'd be covered in blood, sand and scratches from diving around on concrete going for catches. We'd get a shoe box, fill it with sand and put stumps on the top for the wicket. My mum would come looking for me to get me to come home and do my studies. They were happy times alright.'

The contrast between the child-like joy he recalls at just being able to play the game he loves and the sadness he expresses at being driven out of the sport by racism is deeply upsetting. But he's adamant that this must not be seen as just a Yorkshire problem.

'This problem is everywhere,' he argues. 'I have spoken to lots of people from players to coaching and admin level and it's the same story being repeated all over. The only thing that's different is that no one wants to put their head above the parapet. And why would you? It's stressful.'

That is some understatement and a quietness descends on the room after I ask him how he's coping with the pressure.

'The fear is real,' he says after a pause. 'I'm scared for my life. I'm worried for my family's safety. There are emails I've seen that worry me. People know where I am and that scares me. You're constantly looking over your shoulder. You're dealing with powerful people and I won't back down. I am not sure if I can continue to live in the UK. That's how fearful I am.'

He says many people have told him to back down and enjoy a quiet life, but he feels a sense of responsibility to root prejudice out of the game. 'Who else is going to do it? The only way they will stop me is if they kill me,' he says. 'I've had the ultimate pain. I carried my son from the hospital to the graveyard. Nothing you can do is going to make anything worse for me than that.'

He knows that only two things are going to drive change across cricket – further embarrassment if bad practice is highlighted and financial penalties. And as someone who knows how entrenched the culture is at a professional level, he argues that radical interventions need to be considered.

He suggests that a regulator of some sort is needed, and that unannounced spot checks by people spending some time at the club in a different guise could help expose cultural problems that are well hidden. 'If clubs have a racist culture that can be easily identified then take their funding away,' he argues. 'I tell you they will sort it out in 10 minutes. I can guarantee if I'd gone into a meeting with Yorkshire in 2018 and said if you don't sort this out right now, Sport England will remove your funding, it would have got sorted there and then.'

But, above all, the change that Rafiq desperately wants to see is better representation in the top leadership positions. The new Yorkshire Chair Kamlesh Patel is a start, but he wants to see more 'chairmen, CEOs and people on the board'. But not one token person either.

'I hate tokenism,' he says. 'It gives institutions' cover to say, "How can we be racist when we've got such a person on the board?"' But that one person who goes in doesn't get listened to and ends up getting damaged because the community expects a lot and ends up calling them a sell-out when they're not listened to. But they were used all along.'

He doesn't want to see a surge in people of colour appearing on boards for the sake of it. 'Give them fair opportunities so it's the best person for the job that's appointed,' he argues, citing the case of former West Indian cricketer Otis Gibson being appointed Yorkshire's cricket coach through a blind recruitment process.

'They have just done blind recruitment for the first time at Yorkshire for their coaching and Otis scored the highest on every criteria they had. It just shows that when you get a fair opportunity, the best will come to the top.'

He's not wrong and if we're to break the exclusionary stranglehold holding too many sports back and denying talent in Britain, then the most effective vehicle for change has to be leadership. And a lot more sporting bodies need to follow the example that Rafiq cites.

Analysis of major UK sporting bodies, from Archery GB to the Royal Yachting Association, for example, shows that there is a conspicuous lack of ethnic minority representation in leadership positions everywhere in British sport.

At the time of writing, there were still too many sporting bodies showing a chronic lack of leadership around diversity. British Gymnastics, British Cycling, England Golf, British Ice Skating, Ice Hockey UK, British Rowing, British Swimming, British Showjumping Association and English Amateur Dance Sport Association were all bodies that did not have a single person of colour on their board.

Swimming and cycling are listed among the most popular physical activities in a 2021 YouGov poll, with millions enjoying these sports every week. Yet none of the 12 British Swimming Board members are people of colour and the same applies to the board members of British Cycling. It's hardly surprising then that both these sports have shamefully low participation rates among ethnic minorities. According to Swim England, only 2 per cent of regular swimmers are black and 80 per cent of black children do not go swimming at all. For a sport that's claimed to be the best full body workout for your health, these statistics are shameful. British cycling has an equally ignominious record around diversity and it's well known that the sport has a chronic lack of representation from non-white communities.

The sport's governing body claims it no longer collects figures on ethnicity due to General Data Protection Regulation concerns, but the truth is that it's most likely embarrassed by its lack of diversity – and cycling leaders know there's a problem. 'Diversity within cycling in the UK . . . isn't great,' admits James Scott, Cycling UK's director of behaviour change and development, in what can only be described as a huge understatement.

In 2020, *Cycling Weekly* published survey figures from a sample of 4,614 riders who took part in any type of competitive cycling event over the previous two years. It showed that barely 1 per cent of participants were ethnic minorities.

As Britain's most successful Olympic sport, its bountiful gold medal haul stands in stark contrast to the failed sports participation legacy of the 2012 London Games. A useful starting point to examine cycling's pitiful record in supporting ethnic minorities is the website www.antiracismcycling.com, which was launched by the University of Brighton academic, Dr Marlon Moncrieffe. It documents how an array of outstanding black British riders were shut out of the Olympic movement and notes that, despite British riders having won the Tour de France six times since 2012, there has never been a black British rider at the start of the race.

Moncrieffe's analysis sits awkwardly with another report released during the pandemic from Sustrans and Arup, which shows that, despite low participation rates, some 55 per cent of people from ethnic minority groups who do not currently cycle would like to start. Again, a familiar pattern of talent being locked out, unrealised potential and failed leadership is apparent.

Thankfully, not all sports erect such high barriers to prevent participation. Certainly Britain's most popular sport can rightfully claim to be making significant progress in equality, diversion and inclusion. Some 13.5 million people in England play football regularly and many of the game's leading stars are people of colour. When the England national team reached the final of Euro 2020, the first time it had reached a major tournament final since the 1966 World Cup, more than half of Gareth Southgate's 26-man squad had at least one parent or grandparent born outside the UK. It was the most diverse England team ever.

This reflects a growing trend towards increased diversity in football. Since the Premier League began in 1992, the number of ethnic minority players in the top flight has more than doubled. Star players such as Mohamed Salah, Marcus Rashford, Didier Drogba and Thierry Henry have helped establish English football as a globally diverse brand.

However, despite an explosion of ethnic minority talent finding a platform in English football, this hasn't translated to leadership positions in the game.

At the time of writing, around 30 per cent of professional players are black and yet there are only eight black managers working at the 92 clubs in England's four divisions. A report by MPs from the Digital, Culture, Media and Sport Committee has also noted that 'the fact that no Premier League club and virtually no English Football League club has a black owner, chair or chief executive, is a fundamental inequality at the heart of the game.'

This suggests that while the talent of people of colour on the pitch cannot be denied, it certainly can and often is in the boardrooms and corridors of power off the pitch.

But, while such criticism has fallen on deaf ears in other sports, it's fair to say that the football community are alive to the problem, and initiatives like the Football Diversity Leadership Code, launched in October 2020, are beginning to make a difference.

However, for those with experience of the deep-rooted culture that prevails in football, it's going to take more than a steady beat of diversity mood music to make real change.

Dame Heather Rabbatts was the first woman and person of colour on the FA Board in 150 years, serving as chair of their inclusion advisory board from 2011 to 2018.

She smiles when I ask her about progress in making leadership positions more diverse and notes that football is no different to other industries in that people of colour find it hard to grow in powerful positions.

'I remember Angela Davis saying, "You have to take it down brick by brick" because people in power don't give up willingly,' she says, recalling the American civil rights campaigner.

Consequently, for ethnic minorities to be appointed to positions of power they often have to be so much better than other candidates to ensure there's no room for doubt.

'We have to work harder to survive and to prove ourselves,' she explains. 'Nobody gives you the benefit of the doubt, you have to constantly earn their respect. The burden of everybody of colour is on our shoulders.'

'This is fine if we believe that we are standing on the shoulders of giants. But unless we reach a critical mass like the England football team have, then it will take decades.'

Her experience is also telling in relation to the FA's old blazer brigade. In 2015, Rabbatts was subject to a formal investigation after she criticised an FA disciplinary process that cleared José Mourinho of making discriminatory comments towards Chelsea FC's doctor Eva Carneiro but failed to interview Carneiro as part of the process.

Carneiro subsequently took legal action against Chelsea and won an out of court discrimination settlement after the club apologised 'unreservedly' and admitted that José Mourinho was wrong.

'If you criticise the FA publicly, as I did in relation to Eva Carneiro, you get investigated as I was for speaking up and reprimanded,' Rabbatts recalls.

Like many she's quick to celebrate England's diversity on the pitch but says the fact that 'when you look at the England training camp you see a dugout that is still white' means there's still a long way to go.

'General statements of practice are inadequate,' she warns. 'You need to look at every layer including coaches and break the entourage system, which sees new coaches bring along the people they want to work with, who invariably will look like them.'

Many of Rabbatts' insights ring true to me, particularly her view that the exclusion of people of colour from senior positions often creates an imposter syndrome whereby ethnic minority leaders have to be so much better than the rest to justify their appointment.

This thought remained with me when I sat down with one of English football's most powerful black figures, Maheta Molango, the Chief Executive of the Professional Footballers' Association (PFA).

Admiring the surroundings at their impressive Manchester headquarters, I had taken only a few sips of my coffee when Molango took the opportunity to directly address criticism of his appointment.

'I was selected in a transparent process,' he said, a look of bemusement crossing his face when reminded of the criticism that his 2021 appointment drew.

At the time, there were a number of critical media reports and two of the other shortlisted candidates submitted formal complaints. The former Manchester United player, Gary Neville, who sat on the interview panel described the reaction as being motivated by 'xenophobia'.

'It's clear that football is resisting this appointment through feeding journalists with negative information about this candidate – what he can't do, why he shouldn't be there, the process is wrong,' he said. 'I thought it was an awful reaction.'

It clearly irked Molango too, as he patiently explains the experience he brings to the role and why he was appointed. As a former player he said the PFA recognised that he understood the game and as a former Chief Executive of Real Mallorca they could see he was able to understand what the clubs, who are their employers, think. Furthermore, as a former director for FIFA's club management programme, they could see he understood how organisations work and, as a former employment lawyer, he had skills that were very relevant to working for a big union. When you add to that the fact he speaks five languages, it's absurd to question his suitability for the role. He is certainly more qualified than his predecessor, Gordon Taylor, who was reputed to be the highest paid union official in the world. Molango is reportedly paid a quarter of Taylor's salary.

He is, however, well aware of the political significance of his appointment and says it appeals to his ideal of a meritocracy when 'someone who is the son of a social worker from Congo . . . can make it to the very top level of football'.

Molango comes across as a thoughtful, passionate and smart leader, and he brings a unique perspective to the English game.

'I've always been a foreigner all my life,' he says matter-of-factly. 'My parents were immigrants in Switzerland. Then I was an immigrant in Spain, in Germany and in England.'

However, throughout our interview he's hesitant to speak about racism. 'I'm not going down the race road,' he says. 'It's about meritocracy . . . and working hard and working efficiently,' he argues. 'If you don't put barriers in front of you, but rather accept the competition of competing with others, then if you fail, you fail. You hold your hands up and say, "I tried my best but it didn't work out." In my experience, if in ten times you do this and focus on what you can control then maybe three times you're unlucky, you have a racist in front of you, but it's part of life. But six or seven times it should work out.'

This is not the first time I've heard people of colour who are in powerful leadership positions price in racism as something they can do nothing about. And in this respect, Gareth Southgate is arguably more idealistic about equality and diversity than Molango is.

'I don't want to look at this from a victim perspective, but rather from a positive perspective of taking control of what you can control,' Molango says. 'This is the same mentality I used to ask of players when I was Chief Executive of Mallorca. Don't focus on VAR, don't focus on the ref . . . Yes things will go wrong and the ref will be unfair, but don't focus on that because you're wasting energy on things you can't control. I cannot control an idiot who calls me "monkey". He's just an idiot. I focus on what I can do to give me the best chance of succeeding.'

The need to focus on what you can control becomes a running theme in our conversation and Molango mentions it in relation to several areas where racism is rife. On the subject of social media, for example, he says, '1 per cent of haters' are having their voices amplified because we're giving them too much attention. 'Are they even worth our time?' he asks.

While acknowledging that all racists should be prosecuted, he spends a good part of our interview side-stepping opportunities to confront prejudice, instead preferring to focus on finding ways to circumnavigate this cancer in sport.

I sense some of this is rooted in personal experience – and when I gently prod, he offers a fascinating insight into an experience as a young player which I am sure had a huge influence on his outlook.

'There was one incident when I was still playing in Switzerland when someone racially abused me and my reaction led me to being sent off,' he recalls. 'I got a five-game ban because I punched him and this confirms what I told you before. I was the loser because he abused me and there was no evidence to prove it. I overreacted, got sent off and was unable to play first team football. So someone who's abusing you, does he really deserve one second of your time?'

The frustration in his voice suggests it was a painful experience. It's almost as though this failure to achieve justice by confronting racism is why he's reluctant to do so now.

Not surprising then, he is also not a fan of the Rooney Law, which requires teams to interview ethnic minority candidates for head coaching and senior football jobs. 'Someone needs to be chosen because he's the best candidate not because he's a quota,' he says.

But surely this idealised sense of meritocracy doesn't match up to reality? It may do on the pitch where talented youngsters are given a chance, but in management? Talented young managers aren't getting a chance, and the same mediocre managers continue to get jobs long past their sell-by date.

'Why do you think that is?' he says, smiling and suddenly becoming animated. 'If you have an established manager and I'm the chief executive and I pick the established manager and it goes wrong, then it's *his* problem. But if I pick a young manager who's unknown and it goes wrong then it's *my* problem. A lot of owners and chief executives think selfishly that they're better off continuing with the same old guard. This is the reality.'

When I point out that this is clearly not meritocratic he nods and says it's why we need to welcome new owners into football who combine the right corporate skills with an understanding of what the game means – particularly in terms of giving new talent a chance.

'It's not a shoe factory,' he says, with passion in his voice, 'and that's why the PFA is committed to support the efforts of the Government for football to change the fit and proper test for owners.'

It's the first time in our conversation that he's shown a hint of activism, a sense of wanting to actively drive change.

When we leave and pass pictures of iconic black players such as Viv Anderson, Laurie Cunningham and Cyrille Regis in the hallway, I'm left hoping that Molango will, in time, discover more of an activist voice and employ the considerable skills and experience he has to help talented people of colour attain leadership positions.

'I understand it can be frustrating,' he says, as though sensing my thoughts, 'but if you compare what England is compared to other countries then I can promise you we are miles ahead.'

Maybe so in terms of football. But whataboutism is never a good defence and, as we've seen, there are still far too many areas in British sport where talented people of colour are locked out. I can only see this continuing as long as an obstinate mindset prevails across many of our British sporting institutions, which refuses to appoint people of colour to leadership positions.

After many conversations with sports leaders, both at the grassroots and at elite level, there is one enduring image that stays with me. Whether its tennis, cricket, football, swimming, cycling, or any other sport, all I can think of are the young dreamers. The kids charging towards chalked goals on a gable end, pretending to be the next Olympic champion powering through their Council swimming pool, wickets drawn on lamp posts, municipal courts as Wimbledon, and Yorkshire hills becoming Mont Ventoux. Britain is a country teeming with talent and full of dreamers – and all great nations need dreams.

Dreams point to a desired future and inspire us to try harder and never give up. That's why stories like that of the son of Sierra Leonean immigrants who slept at a tennis centre as a child and grew up to conquer American tennis are vital to inspire new generations. So too are stories like Azeem Rafiq's – a boy born in Karachi, who became the first cricketer of Asian origin and the youngest player in the county's history to captain Yorkshire. Or Maheta Molango's story as the son of a social worker from Congo, who rose to lead one of the most powerful bodies in English football.

Britain needs far more of these stories to inspire the next generation to see the invisible and do the impossible. And we'll continue to let down large parts of the country until we get the leaders we deserve.

3

POLITICS

'I never wanted people to know how scary it really was'

The spectre of racism has long hung over our politics. Throughout history it's been ever-present, appealing to people's worst instincts, dividing communities and playing on fears. And it's one area where no political party can be said to have clean hands. The Tories once famously campaigned under the slogan, 'If you want a n***** as a neighbour, vote Labour', while the trade unions and Labour had difficult relations with migrant workers in the 1960s and 1970s. We shouldn't forget that London dockers once marched with placards that read 'Back Britain, not Black Britain'.

But if the hallmark of twentieth-century racism in politics was direct, unambiguous and ugly sloganeering, the birth of a modern multicultural Britain saw a deft shift in tone. Crude Enoch Powell style 'Rivers of Blood' speeches were out. What became acceptable in politics was what American journalist Ta-Nehisi Coates referred to as 'elegant racism'.

Elegant racism, explained Coates, was invisible because it disguised itself in the national discourse. Instead of crude epithets, it would hide behind voter ID laws. Or, in Britain, behind 'hostile environment' policies to tackle illegal immigration. These aimed to make life so unbearable for undocumented immigrants that they would voluntarily choose to leave.

This policy, announced under the Coalition Government in 2012, turned all sorts of professionals, from doctors and teachers to landlords and police, into immigration enforcers. One minister was said to have warned at the time that 'anyone foreign looking' would face challenges accessing private rented accommodation. But the Government ploughed on. And by extending immigration control away from Government officials into the heart of every community, it would hugely overreach with devastating consequences.

This fundamental flaw meant that some communities, who were not targets of the policy, and had legitimate immigration status, would suffer immensely. Many of the Windrush generation, now in their sixties and seventies, who arrived in Britain between 1948 and 1970 from the Caribbean and other Commonwealth countries to address post-war labour shortages, lacked the documentation to prove their right to stay in the UK. Consequently, many of them lost jobs, homes and access to NHS treatment, and were forcibly deported to countries they left as children.

When I spoke to Amber Rudd, the Home Secretary who oversaw this scandal, and was subsequently forced to resign in 2018, she said she'd thought long and hard about racism in public life.

While acknowledging that 'constant vigilance is needed to avoid it', she conceded that a failure to embrace diverse leadership resulted in ignorant policy-making.

'As Wendy Williams' independent review showed, ignorance played a large part in the Windrush scandal,' she explains. 'I agree with her that understanding the history of the UK's immigration policy is important for people in the Home Office so they are fair.

'But it's not enough to have a diversity policy. We have to have really diverse workforces. So often the public sector responds by quoting a figure which looks reassuring, but in fact has very few senior people working at the top. That needs to change.'

Change was certainly in the air in 2016 when Amber Rudd became Home Secretary. But not of the kind she recognises is needed now. The 'elegant racism' that Coates once referred to was beginning to be tested. For years dog whistle politics had been a central part of British politics – exemplified by Conservative posters in 2005 emblazoned with the slogan, 'Are you thinking what we're thinking?'

But now dog whistles were becoming bolder. They would ultimately lose any coded or suggestive language to become racist air horns, as Nigel Farage's 'Breaking Point' poster showed. But in the early months of 2016, there was little sign of the deep racial fissures that would soon be exposed.

In January, the Prime Minister wrote the following in the *Sunday Times*: 'When you look at Britain today, it is much harder to see the open discrimination and blatant racism of decades gone by. Instead there is a grown-up country that, despite our challenges, is largely at ease with the diversity of our open society.'

Around the same time, the London mayoral contest between Labour's Sadiq Khan and the Conservative Party's Zac Goldsmith was starting to heat up.

With Khan moving into an early lead, it didn't take long before the Tory campaign decided to go negative and drop any belief they had of a grown-up country at ease with diversity. Even by normal standards of what's euphemistically referred to as 'the cut and thrust' of politics, this would plumb new depths. In a harbinger of what was to come in the Brexit referendum, it shamelessly exploited racial divisions to become one of the dirtiest campaigns in living memory.

'At every opportunity they implied I was a terrorist,' explains Khan when we met, six years after he became London's first ethnic minority mayor.

As I listen to him recounting the hatred thrown at him, there's a mixture of incredulity and resignation in his voice. Even now, he seems baffled that Zac Goldsmith, who he'd previously described as 'charming' and someone who celebrated the diversity of London, would want to bet everything on a racist campaign, aided and abetted by the Prime Minister and Home Secretary. But in the summer of 2015, this was a portent of what was to come.

'During the selection campaign to be the Labour candidate, I wasn't the favourite. Tessa Jowell was the favourite,' recalls Khan. 'I was fourth favourite, but making progress. Then LBC did a poll asking if Londoners would be comfortable with a Muslim mayor. Not, "Wouldn't it be great for London to have a Muslim mayor?" but, "Would you be comfortable with a Muslim mayor?"' He says the words slowly and deliberately and it's the only time in our interview that he sounds angry.

'Of course the numbers weren't great for obvious reasons,' he adds (almost a third said they would not want to be led by a man of Islamic faith). 'I had volunteers on my campaign turning up the next day in tears because they felt, "Why are we doing this? What's the point?"'

But Khan won and his candidacy inspired many across London and the rest of the country. Here was someone who would not only become a global symbol of London's diversity and integration, but, as the son of a Pakistani bus driver, was the living embodiment of the immigration success story and visible social mobility.

However, his candidacy also inspired some of the vilest emotions, and his opponent was determined to try and mobilise them against Khan. Newspaper articles began to appear with pictures of Khan next to a destroyed double decker bus from the 7/7 bombings. At every step elements of the media tried to exploit anti-Muslim hatred and link his candidacy to the threat of terrorism. 'On Thursday, are we really going to hand the world's greatest city to a Labour party that thinks terrorists are its friends?'

headlined an opinion piece by Zac Goldsmith in the *Mail on Sunday*.

The terrible irony is that Khan has frequently been a target for extremists and once had a Fatwa issued against him for voting to introduce Equal Marriage.

Looking back on his historic campaign, Khan understandably has mixed emotions. It was undoubtedly an incredible, exhilarating period where hope ultimately prevailed. But it was also one that took a heavy toll on him and his campaign team. Subsequent events have made him question whether more British Muslims have been turned off from entering politics as a result.

'At the beginning of the campaign, I had dozens of mums, dads, aunties, uncles, grandads and grannies coming up to me saying, "We're really proud you're running, my kids are so excited. They want to be politicians now",' he remembers. 'But towards the end of the campaign, I had people coming to me saying, "You know what, we've thought about it and after what you've been through we're discouraging our kids, nephews and nieces from being politicians." And this is the reason why I don't like talking about what I've gone through because I don't want to put off kids from being politicians.'

His reluctance to speak of his experience of being the only mayor in the country to require round-the-clock police protection is a constant source of torment. On the one hand, I can see he wants to inspire other British Asians from working-class backgrounds to pursue political careers and be elected to high office. But he also can't hide the toxic reality of being in the cross hairs 24/7.

First elected as an MP for Tooting in 2005, Khan's experience is a lesson in what some people of colour in public life have to endure. He says he's always been conscious of 'being different' and speaks eloquently about the politics of racial identity that have shaped his journey.

Growing up, he says, racial abuse was common and he was involved in a lot of fights as a teenager. 'It was a red flag,' he says.

'If someone used a term of racial abuse, there was a fight. Those were the rules of the game.' He was chased away by the National Front when he went to see football matches at Chelsea and Wimbledon and ended up supporting Liverpool as a result. When he went to support England at a test match against Pakistan at Lords aged 12 he was, again, on the receiving end of vile racist abuse from England fans.

When he grew older, he describes seeing people become politicised in terms of religion at university during the Salman Rushdie affair and the first Gulf War. 'You noticed people looked at you differently and this was before 9/11, which changed everything.'

When he stood to become MP, he was much more aware of how 'othering' was affecting his progress. 'I was repeatedly asked questions by Labour members (many who had known me since I joined the party at 15) on my views on abortion, faith schools, homosexuality and head scarves,' he remembers. 'After I won, I asked the other candidates if they had been asked questions like this and none of them had.'

As an MP he immediately noticed he was at a disadvantage because he didn't drink. 'Your networks are made in the Strangers' Bar in Westminster, they're made when you go for a drink with general secretaries in a pub and I was excluded from that drinking culture,' he observes.

He describes this loss of social capital as 'a lack of glue that people have as part of a tribe', but this exclusion extended to him not even being recognised as an individual. 'I was often called Shahid, Mr Vaz, Mr Mahmood or Marsha by security, other MPs and staff at the House of Commons,' he says. 'On one occasion someone called me Mr Khabra, a full year after the MP for Ealing Southall, Piara Khabra had died!'

When questioned as to whether he thinks similar cases of 'othering' still go on today in Westminster, he's quick to explain a key factor in how people of colour are viewed. 'There's the assimilation school of thought and the integration school of thought,' he notes.

The assimilation model sees immigrants jump into the melting pot, adopt the majority culture, drink and do all the stuff that the majority of people do and anglicise your name.

'I've never assimilated,' he says. 'I've integrated and what that means is I'm still very much a Muslim. I practise my faith and fast during Ramadan. I know I've missed out because I'm an integrationist rather than an assimilator.'

To compensate he says he's had to work a lot harder than many of his peers and insists there's an important difference in not just being an ethnic minority, but a religious minority too.

The fact that the religion he belongs to is constantly cited in research and surveys as being the one subject to most prejudice in Britain has only made his journey harder and meant he's constantly viewed with suspicion.

When he went to visit his constituent Babar Ahmad, who was the longest serving prisoner to be detained without trial in the UK, in Woodhill Prison, for example, he was bugged by Scotland Yard without his knowledge.

Khan was understandably furious at what happened, not least because the code known as the Wilson doctrine forbids the covert recording of discussions between MPs and their constituents. But he added that the most depressing repercussion was that the actions of police were used as a recruiting tool for extremists.

Hizb ut-Tahir and others subsequently used this fact to try and radicalise people, he explains. 'They said, "If Sadiq Khan the Labour MP is being bugged, do you wonder why we want a caliphate?"'

As Khan rose through the political ranks, first as a local Government minister and then becoming the first ever Muslim to join the cabinet as the Minister of State for Transport, he understandably began to attract more attention.

By the time he became the first Muslim mayor of a major Western capital city, he was valuable currency as clickbait in a hate-filled, algorithm-driven new digital world.

As soon as prominent commentators posted something criticising him on social media, Khan's name would act as a lightning rod for torrents of abuse, death threats and vile racism.

His staff at City Hall had to be offered counselling as a result of the deluge of abusive emails and letters they received that were directed at him.

Khan saw the link between social media and sickening abuse in the spike of hate mail that his office would receive when prominent figures attacked him. Famously, in a keynote speech at the 2018 South by Southwest music, film and interactive media festival in Texas, he read out some of the tweets he receives.

'Muslims have no dignity. I wish Sadiq Khan would blow himself up like they all do. He might get his 12 virgins.'

'I say kill the Mayor of London and you will be rid of one Muslim terrorist.'

'I'd pay for someone to execute Sadiq Khan.'

But the tweets that arguably did him the most harm were those from the world's most notorious tweeter, President Donald Trump.

Their Twitter spat started in 2016 and ran on for years with Trump referring to Khan as a 'stone cold loser' and 'a disaster'. In 2019, Trump tweeted that 'London needs a new mayor ASAP' and that Khan was 'a national disgrace who is destroying the city of London'.

'What most people don't know,' says Khan looking back, 'is that every time he did a tweet, City Hall was bombarded with threatening emails and messages, and my social media was full of hate.'

Social media would have a lasting effect on Khan's safety and he says it took him a while to realise the impact it could have.

'After a few months of being elected [as mayor] the police said I should have protection and I refused,' he says. 'The police had seen the traffic and they were doing risk assessments. But it was only in March 2017 when things started to get really bad that I realised I had a duty of care towards my family and staff, so I agreed.'

As a keen sports fan, Khan admits to following the old boxing adage of not letting your opponent know when you're hurt or tired.

'We all do it. I've never wanted people to know how scary it was,' he says, his voice freighted with sorrow. 'You're the first person I'm speaking to who I'm admitting it was scary. You had Donald Trump basically being incredibly nasty in a personal way about me and . . . well . . . I'm just the Mayor of London. I'm not the President of Russia, I'm not the Prime Minister of India or the President of Iran. I'm just a mayor trying to sort out public transport, housing and so forth. It was scary, it was personal and it was poison. A combination of Brexit and Trump brought things to the surface that we thought had long been put to bed.'

Of all the conversations I had with people in politics for this book, Khan's candid admission of feeling scared by racist attacks troubled me most. The Mayor of London has been subject to considerable media criticism for being driven around in a mayoral motorcade. He's been mocked for not following the example of his predecessor, who was frequently seen riding a bike to City Hall. Yet very few know the real reasons why two leaders in the same job took such a different approach to travel.

Khan's story is sadly far from unique, though. Over 200 miles away in Oldham, north Manchester, I heard a similar tale of fear and loathing.

In May 2021, Councillor Arooj Shah became Oldham's first Muslim female Council leader in a town that has a history of racial tensions. Twenty years earlier, police officers had faced a hail of petrol bombs, bricks and bottles in what was described as the worst ethnically motivated riots in the UK since 1985. The rioting started in Glodwick, one of the country's poorest wards, where Shah has lived all her life.

Cars were torched, young people clashed with police and a local pub was firebombed after an argument between a group of Asian boys playing cricket and two white children spiralled out of control. When carloads of white men arrived shortly afterwards and began attacking Asian people at random, rioting quickly spread across the town.

A year later the openly racist British National Party would secure 12,000 votes in Oldham.

I sat down with Shah in early 2022, fully aware that she has one of the most challenging political jobs in Greater Manchester.

Not only is she grappling with the problems associated with one of the most deprived towns here, but she's also having to manage constant attacks that threaten her personal safety.

Tears run down Shah's face as she recounts how, only a few months after she'd taken on the leadership role, flames leapt into the air once more, as her car was firebombed.

'That felt deeply personal,' she recalls, her voice faltering. 'It was hate and somebody could have gone further and not wanted me around. And then I thought, has someone been watching me for days because I tend to finish conversations [on my phone] in the car? I had to hide my feelings and pretend that I could deal with it because you're in a position of leadership and that's what's expected of you. But it felt so traumatic.

'I've become half the person I was since I became leader and I've never felt so brown. I've never felt such an imposter because it doesn't matter who you are or what your beliefs are, to the world you're a brown woman and you don't belong here. So I have to work 50 times harder. If I do something that people don't agree with it's always, "Oh, it's that Muslim leader". It's really difficult because I was born and raised here, I love this town, it's mine and I want to do the best for all of us.'

In the course of our conversation, she repeats that chilling phrase over and over.

'I've never felt so brown.'

Each time it makes me wince. We live in an age where, on the face of it, Britain has never been more comfortable with diversity. No major business worth its salt doesn't have a Diversity and Inclusion strategy these days. No corporate website is complete without pictures of racially diverse people. And from Disney to Netflix, films are tripping over themselves to celebrate black and Asian culture.

But still, in the world of politics, far too many towns remain uncomfortable at the prospect of a brown, woman leader.

When she stood for leadership of the Labour group in Oldham, and therefore the Council as Labour is the largest party, Shah says discussions didn't focus on her values or politics. They were about her skin colour, religion and sex.

As leader, she admits it has been an uphill struggle to get things done and describes it as a lonely place.

'On Remembrance Sunday this year I stood at Oldham Cenotaph and, despite attending that ceremony many times, I felt something new – I felt fear. I was scared to look at the faces of the people in the crowd in case I saw hate; I was scared to walk through town alone afterwards in case someone approached me aggressively. And that's what being leader has taken away from me – it's taken my sense of safety.'

She recalls watching, from the position of deputy, as the previous Council leader made changes and decisions that went unquestioned and were swiftly actioned. Her experience has been very different.

She talks about asking for additional investment for cleaning streets, tackling fly-tipping and enforcing against those who dump waste. A simple enough request you'd think, but one that she received considerable push back on.

'I was asked if I had thought about "how things might look" if I chose to invest additional money in cleaning streets [the implication being more would be spent in predominantly Pakistani and Bangladeshi areas of the borough].'

'And it's that sense, that everything I do has to be viewed through a lens of race, that is most frustrating and most dangerous. If I ask the Government to consider additional support during the height of the pandemic for those self-isolating who were self-employed, it's assumed I mean this only to benefit Asian taxi drivers. If I advocate for understanding from the community around asylum placements in the borough I am accused of building a Muslim caliphate in the town. I am relentlessly accused of benefiting from "block postal votes" and covering up child sexual abuse from "my own community" in exchange for these votes.'

As well as her car being firebombed, Shah has had multiple death threats, and faces online abuse every day; when out canvassing or visiting residents she's often threatened in the streets by people who believe she promotes terrorism.

When I ask her the last time she was abused, she says a few days ago she was out canvassing when a man answered the door and told her he couldn't possibly vote Labour. She politely asked why and was told 'because your party has too many people like *you*.'

There's sadness in her eyes as she shares this experience. 'He said it to my face,' she adds, and you can hear the pain in her voice. 'We're a diverse town and it shouldn't be shocking that we have a Muslim leader because you have to represent the communities you serve.'

But, sadly, in many areas it does still shock people. From Oldham to Bradford and Sheffield to Dewsbury, there's a wealth of ethnically diverse communities. But Shah remains the first Muslim woman to take charge of a Council in the north of England.

'What makes the job really difficult is we have a culture that isn't there to receive it yet,' she argues, 'and that's where the problem is.'

I've long known that the best local politicians develop a strong antennae for danger and hate – and Shah was certainly not exaggerating.

As this book went to press, she narrowly lost her seat in the May local elections after an extremely negative campaign. Given that her party was making gains everywhere across England, as the Government were struggling with multiple scandals, it was a result that spoke volumes. Shah was right in saying the culture wasn't there to accept a female Muslim leader – and that was made clear in the ugliest terms.

'It was a personal campaign and they dehumanised me completely,' she told her local newspaper. 'My mum was horrified and scared for my wellbeing.'

I spoke to countless politicians when writing this book to try and learn more about Shah's observation that the wrong culture was in place to receive people of colour as leaders.

Many said there were fears about how it would play with voters, and others pointed to Zac Goldsmith's campaign as a reason why there was nervousness about pushing ethnic minority leaders.

But one former Asian Conservative Party parliamentary candidate, who asked to remain anonymous, said there were many other factors to consider.

'It's not like everyone with a black or brown skin will have the same experience in any political party, particularly the Tory party,' he says. 'I think class and your educational and family background is an important determinant. I'm sure someone like Shaun Bailey, for example, has had a very different experience of the Tory Party than an Etonian like Kwasi Kwarteng.'

Pointing to his own experience, he said he wasn't as well connected as someone like Rishi Sunak and not only had to fight a difficult seat but was often treated as though he was 'fresh off the boat'.

He added that there was a lack of understanding of ethnic minority communities too, noting that he was once asked to stand in an area where there was a big Asian community. 'But it was a large Sikh community and I'm Muslim. It showed their ignorance. For them it was just brown people,' he said.

It wasn't until 2005 that the first black Tory MP, Adam Afriyie, was elected and our parliamentary candidate admits that, in the early 2000s, the Tories were desperate to shake off an image of being too pale, male and stale.

'Michael Howard could see Blair with all these people of colour and he had no one,' he explains. 'So I had a call from the party saying they wanted articulate Muslims, but it smacked of a colonial mentality to me. They just wanted an articulate brown person to stand next to them and make them look good. This was after 7/7 and I didn't want to be the "articulate Muslim" who would be wheeled out in front of the cameras to speak about "Muslim issues". I never wanted to go into politics to promote race or Muslim issues. Some people go into politics to champion their religious community, but that wasn't for me.'

Howard's drive sounds a lot like tokenism to me and when I ask if the culture in the party is more supportive of diversity these days, he's not entirely sure. 'A lot of Conservative associations are looking for a prospective son-in-law rather than a candidate,' he says dryly. 'I told the party to stop putting people of colour in heavily dominated ethnic minority areas, which is what they did back then. The problem was ethnic minorities hated them. I argued that if they were serious about transforming the image of the party they had to start putting minorities in super safe shire seats where they will win – and this is exactly what they did with Sajid Javed, Nadhim Zahawi and others. But back then it was hard to get a safe seat.'

Looking back, he says his experience of contesting a marginal seat would be enough to put most people off running for public office – particularly as he had hardly any support from the party.

'Campaigning is hard and people can be very nasty,' he recalls. 'I remember someone screaming in my face in the town centre. He was so close to me spit was flying out of his mouth and I was covered in his saliva. It was awful. I remember afterwards when I lost by a few thousand votes, having busted my backside for two years in this place, going to one of my supporters to take a poster board down from his house and to thank him for his support.

'They were this supposedly decent English couple and he said to me, "You know, with hindsight we should have picked a standard candidate." I looked at him and said, "What do you mean?" and he replied, "A white male".'

And therein lies the rub. Subconsciously the default image of the white male is inextricably bound up in power. 'If you are a default man,' argues artist, writer and broadcaster Grayson Perry, 'you *look* like power.'

This conditioned image of the white male as being most suited to lead is something Ijeoma Oluo explores powerfully in her book, *Mediocre*. She argues that 'a deliberate building of white male identity' has created norms that reward mediocre white men. Conversely, as interviews for this book demonstrated, women and ethnic minorities often struggle to be accepted – or *seen* – as leaders.

It's not just politics where this is a challenge, though. It's also an issue in the routes into power and among critical stakeholders.

As the first black President of Wales TUC and the Welsh Government Minister for Economy, Vaughan Gething is clear that Westminster is not the only institution that needs a cultural re-boot.

'You have to look at how you are as an employer and trade unions need to look at why their pipeline is so white,' he tells me.

The MP for Brent Central, Dawn Butler, is another key figure who has been outspoken on structural inequalities. As the third black woman ever to be elected as an MP, and also the first ever elected female African-Caribbean minister to speak at the Dispatch Box, Butler says she's had to struggle with being accepted as a politician.

'In Westminster, I have been mistaken for a cleaner getting into an MPs-only lift. I have been confronted about whether I should be allowed onto an MPs-only area on the terrace. These things happen all the time. Sometimes, I feel exhausted and don't have the energy to deal with it. Other days, I feel angry and I know I have to challenge it.

'But always, in every instance, I ask myself when is this going to change?'

Butler is certainly not on her own in sharing these frustrations.

Previously described by *The Voice* newspaper as 'the most senior Asian lady in the BBC', Anjula Singh's switch from Deputy Head of Production Operations to become Director of Communications for the Labour Party was hailed as a serious move to help the party achieve more success with broadcast media.

But having led large production departments and managed a £25 million budget at the BBC, she says her success has been a prolonged struggle.

'My experience has always been the same – I have had to be at least 10 times as good as others to be recognised for my work,' she explains. 'I have earnt each promotion through relentless delivery, unlike my male, white, privately educated [and mainly Oxbridge] counterparts who merely need to show promise, sit back in their chairs taking up more space than is really necessary, think big thoughts and talk a lot.'

This very much characterises her experience in politics, where she says she found it difficult to be accepted and frequently felt like an outsider.

'The mainly white men I worked with in politics had difficulty accepting my leadership and respecting my experience or skills,' she reflects. 'They were from the most privileged backgrounds with elite education and built-in generational advantages. They have never had to work alongside anyone of colour, let alone be led by them. I admired their brains but also wondered what my brain could be like if I had grown up with access to the same privileges.

'On one occasion, because a male colleague didn't like what I was saying, I had someone physically jump up and down clenching his fists like a toddler and kicking the sofa which was next to me. He got even more angry when I told him that was unacceptable workplace behaviour and asked him how he would respond if I had behaved as he had.'

This picture of entitlement is an apt metaphor for our political institutions.

And a reminder of how the culture in politics remains far from inclusive.

Whether it's Bullingdon Club bad behaviour, beer and sandwiches machismo or a continuing conveyor belt of Oxbridge PPE educated clones, too much of our politics is saturated in a narrow and elitist culture that's unwelcoming to diverse talent.

We have one of the oldest and most mature democracies in the world but it's still rooted in an outdated 'clubby' culture that plumps for tokenism over genuine diversity.

Changing this at a time when our politicians have never been held in lower esteem is not going to be easy. Perhaps then, it's right to give the last word to Sadiq Khan, a politician who knows better than most why so many people of colour have been turned off from pursuing a career in politics.

'We have to let people be themselves!' he exclaims. 'It's the integration versus assimilation point and what price do we have to pay? If we allow people to be themselves that will cast the talent net further.'

He does, however, remain optimistic about the future.

'One of the things that gives me hope is Liverpool Football Club,' he adds with a smile. 'It's a fact that when John Barnes played, people threw bananas at him. But Mohamed Salah and Sadio Mane have done more to educate football fans about racism than anyone else. Fans now sing positive songs about him being a Muslim and going to the mosque. They are amazing and we have to be talking up these successes. When Salah scores and does the sujood it's brilliant.'

As the parent of a Liverpool-supporting son, I've seen thousands of fans singing these songs on the terraces. One of them is sung to Dodgy's "Good Enough", and the lyrics are:

'If he's good enough for you, he's good enough for me.
If he scores another few, then I'll be Muslim too.
If he's good enough for you, he's good enough for me.
Sitting in the mosque, that's where I wanna be!
Mo Salah-la-la-la, la-la-la-la-la-la-la.'

Khan certainly makes an interesting point here. In 2021, research published in the *American Political Science Review* showed that after Salah joined Liverpool Football Club, hate crimes in the Liverpool area dropped by 16 per cent and that his performances enabled positive feelings towards Salah to generalise to Muslims more broadly. The research also showed that Liverpool fans halved their rates of posting anti-Muslim tweets relative to fans of other top-flight clubs.

But it's not just Salah's goal-scoring feats that should be celebrated, explains Khan. He talks of a genuinely inclusive culture at the club where players avoid spraying the doctor with champagne after winning because they know he's a Muslim and that the manager allows Mane and Salah to train at different times when they're fasting. He argues that it's the culture that has allowed him to be himself and reach his full potential.

It certainly begs a serious question. If this can be achieved on the fields of Anfield Road, why is it so hard for a similar culture to be adopted in the halls of Westminster and in town halls across the country?

4

FILM & CULTURE

Love Thy Neighbour

What we must remember is that 1970s' Britain is unrecognisable from the country we live in today. Ostensibly, people of colour have greater protection in law than ever before. Those who accuse us of being in the era of 'woke', where white people are muzzled, argue that the law has gone too far, and the scales of justice have tilted against the 'indigenous' folk of the UK.

However, I use the word 'ostensibly' deliberately. We are *supposed* to have greater protection. Yet, post-George Floyd, and with the recent label of 'structural and systemic racism' to add to institutional racism, what has changed?

Of course, the truthful answer is an enormous amount from when I was a boy growing up in Birmingham. Let me be clear: Britain remains a wonderful country of true opportunity. And when we British citizens of colour criticise our home, our patriotism should not be questioned. We are part of its history, its present and its future, whether you like it or not. Through literal blood, sweat and tears, our great-great-grand parents (we are entering our fifth established generation since the mass influx in the 1960s) downwards have made the UK what it is today. Lest we forget, being part of the Empire meant we were British and so Britain was 'our home'. Indeed, the 1948 Act gave Commonwealth citizens the automatic right to settle. Something conveniently forgotten when we are accused of being *immigrants*, a word that's become short-hand for 'foreigners who don't belong here, who come here to steal our jobs, our homes and our women'.

When I was growing up, suspicion of those arriving, often with just three pounds in their pockets, to fill the factory jobs, work in the NHS, drive the buses and clean the toilets, which many Britons refused to do, was reflected on our screens.

In the 1970s, Britain had just three national channels: BBC 1, BBC 2 and ITV. We would have to wait until 1982 for Channel 4 and 1997 for Channel 5, in terms of terrestrial stations. Actually, the revolution for choice via satellite started on 5 February 1989, when Rupert Murdoch launched Sky in the UK. The Australian newspaper tycoon had been broadcasting in Europe five years earlier.

Today on the front page of its website, the broadcaster declares, 'Sky is Europe's leading media and entertainment company, and we are proud to be part of Comcast Corporation.'

'Across six countries our innovative products connect 23 million customers to the best apps, and all the entertainment, sports, news and arts they love, including our own award-winning original content.'

But in the 1970s, playgrounds were abuzz with whatever was peak-time viewing on those three channels, and therein lay the problem. Speak to anyone of colour alive at that time, and you would be hard pressed to find anyone who thought our television stations represented them.

Of course, the BBC with its public service remit ensured we 'immigrants', arriving in our thousands, had *Nai Zindagi Naya Jeevan* on a Sunday. The programme, presented by Mahendra Kaul and Saleem Shahed, the only brown faces on UK television, started in 1968 and stopped broadcasting in 1982. Every Sunday morning thousands of us would be glued around the Bakelite black-and-white television sets. For most of us, this would be the only TV we kids would be allowed to watch.

As a rather funny aside, *Nai Zindagi Naya Jeevan* was a peculiar title for the show. Translated from its Hindi and Urdu into English it means 'New Way, New Life.' I suspect what the BBC wanted it to say was *New Life, New Beginnings*, in which case it should have been *Naya Jeevan/Zindagi Naee Shuruaat*. Perhaps the south Asians who may have helped come up with the title did so deliberately, and they wanted their immigrant brothers and sisters to realise there was no real life in the UK.

But all this was irrelevant to most people, as the highlights of 1970s' television were programmes such as *Till Death Us Do Part*, with the racist Alf Garnett and a browned-up Spike Milligan; *It Ain't Half Hot Mum* with its browned-up Michael Bates, and cough-hacking punkah-wallahs; *Mind Your Language* with a class which introduced us to wobble-heads; *Mixed Blessings* and its depiction of a mixed-race marriage (this most certainly wasn't *Guess Who's Coming To Dinner*); and, of course, *Love Thy Neighbour*, which showed the male partners in two couples – one black, the other racist white – at war with one another.

We should not forget *The Fosters*, the forerunner to *Desmond's* in the 1980s, based on the American sit-com *Good Times*, which introduced us to Sir Lenny Henry's superb acting talents. It was the first ever show where all the main characters were black.

Henry makes no secret of his discomfort of appearing in a staple of British television since 1958, *The Black and White Minstrel Show*. Here, white men would 'black up'. Mind you they were not alone. Anyone wishing to play Shakespeare's *Othello* or the Prince of Morocco in *The Merchant of Venice* would have to be played by a white actor with black or brown shoe polish layering his face.

Henry himself was the product of the television talent show, *New Faces*. His Frank Spencer impression was to die for. The young boy from Dudley, which was near to where I grew up, blossomed before our very eyes. But if you were to go back and look at that first appearance, almost every joke, in front of an all-white audience, was making fun of his skin colour, something he highlighted when he was the subject of Alan Yentob's *Imagine* series on BBC 1 in 2020. It was his way of protecting himself, 'get it in first, before they do,' he told Yentob. By his own admission, that appearance on *New Faces*, that ability to win over and be accepted by white people, kept him employed for the next 10 years. In the past, the entertainer has said that the media operated a 'one-in-one-out rule', where only one person of colour could ever be in one television or radio show. To be fair to him, in the past decade Henry has been at the forefront of campaigning for racial equality in the industry.

Racial insensitivity continued for decades in the media, and if truth be told, it still exists today. But, for the moment, let us concentrate on the 'early days'. In the 1986 series, *Lord Mountbatten: The Last Viceroy*, we had Ian Richardson playing Jawaharlal Nehru, India's first Prime Minister; his white colleague Sam Dastor browned-up in his role as Mahatma Gandhi; and the producers cast Polish-born actor Vladek Sheybal as Muhammad Ali Jinnah, known as Quaid-i-Azam [Great Leader], revered by Pakistanis across the globe as the father of the nation.

In 2021, Henry told *The Times*, 'I had become a political football. My way through all of this was to bury my head in the sand and let any controversy wash over me.' Shamefully, the BBC used the fact he was in *The Black and White Minstrel Show* to defend a complaint to the Race Relations Board that it was racist.

The big problem about television in the 1970s, 1980s and parts of the 1990s is that conscious and deliberate racism took place masked in the name of comedy. It was acceptable to use words such as 'coon', 'wog', 'Paki' and 'nig-nog'. It was acceptable for white actors to put towels on their heads, wobble their heads, and try to imitate the south Asian accents. It was acceptable for south Asian and black communities to be stereotyped as lazy, dirty, smelly, sly scroungers who always wanted to cheat the white men and women heroes of Great Britain.

Why did this happen? Because all the commissioners were white, and they were mainly men, who never had a clue what happened the night after *Love Thy Neighbour* and its ilk aired.

In the playgrounds the next day, south Asians and black children would be welcomed with 'Alright Sambo?' or 'Get out of the way, you dirty smelly wog.' It was not just verbal. Our experiences of living through the recurrent and frequent episodes of 'Paki-bashing' are things etched into our memories, never far from the surface.

We rarely talk about these to our white colleagues, but in homes across Britain, south Asians of a certain age thank God our children and grandchildren do not have to face the hostility we did, made worse by the lack of representation on screen.

It was not until 1998 that Britain was introduced to authentic south Asian humour. Thanks to Sanjeev Bhaskar, Meera Syal, Nina Wadia and Kulvinder Ghir, we let out a secret we south Asians had kept for decades. We have a great sense of humour. Not only that, we could, with great authenticity, take the proverbial out of ourselves, and we did not need white people browned-up to show off our talent.

'Kiss my chuddis' [underpants], 'going for an English', everything being of Indian origin, are now part and fabric of British comedy and British vernacular. *Goodness Gracious Me* started life on radio, and it was so funny that the BBC allowed it to move to television.

A quick aside. In the 1990s Sanjeev was part of a comedy duo with his long-time friend, the musician Nitin Sawhney, called *The Secret Asians*. The former BBC Head of Religion Aaqil Ahmed started his corporation career working on *Bollywood or Bust*, a Saturday quiz show for south Asians. It was he who brought Sanjeev to host the programme.

Ahmed told the newspaper, *Eastern Eye*, that Bhaskar confided in him about *Goodness Gracious Me*, to which he responded, 'Don't be silly. Asian comedy show. Never happen and won't last. Well, thank goodness he ignored me. What do I know?'

And Ahmed was not alone. Sanjeev recalled that the BBC did not exactly welcome him with open arms.

'I knew a producer, Anil Gupta, who had conversations with my Mrs, Meera [Syal], because they had both been working on *The Real McCoy*, which was a black British sketch show, and Meera said "I think we've got enough material to do our own show."

'Anil went to the BBC and said we'd like to put on a comedy. They said, and this was the question asked of me from journalists when the show first came out, "Are Asians funny?"

'I said we've been funny for 5,000 years, but we have had no need to tell you before, but we're telling you now.'

That sense of having to prove yourself more than the white person is nothing new. We live with it. We accept it. We let it drive us.

'The BBC gave us six days to come up with a live show from scratch. So, we all met on a Monday, and on Saturday we performed this show for about an hour or so,' said Bhaskar.

'The purse string holders at the BBC sent someone who said afterwards, "I don't get it but obviously the audience does. So why don't we try a radio pilot?"

'We'd gone in there thinking we had a TV show but he said you can do a radio pilot, so we did that, got it on the radio.'

Not only do people of colour have to prove ourselves, we have to go above and beyond the norm.

'We said, "Now can we do the TV show?" They said, "No, you can do a TV pilot."

'So, we did a TV pilot and then they said this is great, we'll do a series and put it out at around 11 o'clock on a Wednesday night.

'And I said, "Why then? Is that Asian prime time when they've closed their shops? It's a very British format."'

One thing we people of colour have learnt is that we cannot be angry. Bhaskar had one thing we all need – humour with a message.

'I vaguely remember an executive bringing a chair across the room and it ended up on Friday night at 11 o'clock.'

'I don't know of any other comedy group that had to jump through that many hoops.

'We were given six days and 10 grand to come up with a live show, do a radio pilot, then do a radio series which won an award, then do a TV pilot, then do a TV show.'

Bhaskar remains convinced that despite the successes, it was his colour which – and this will sound funny considering how well he has done – held him back.

'The other comedy shows at the time, none of them were brown, but none of them had any more experience than us collectively,' he explained.

'I had no experience, this was my first thing. But Meera was quite established, Anil was a producer at the BBC anyway, two of the other writers were a writing team that had written on other shows.

'The other sketch shows or comedy groups that got on . . . that [colour] was the only difference.'

For those who have not experienced what is now referred to as 'unconscious bias' but is in fact plain, simple racism, this may be hard to understand. It will come across as one of Britain's biggest talents whinging, making excuses, and being completely ungrateful to an industry which has made him a star and household name. But he is not alone.

Shobna Gulati is an amazing actress who knows that by speaking out she may do damage to her career. She is probably best known for her five-year role as Sunita Alahan in *Coronation Street*. But she burst onto our screen in Victoria Wood's *Dinnerladies*. The fact that people of colour are treated differently from white thespians is something Gulati learnt early in her career.

'I trained in Indian dance and received a fellowship from the Arts Council of England when I was at the onset of my career,' she remembered.

'I was on placement with the Royal Ballet. It was obvious that the woman in charge of the "education and learning" department had a problem with me.

'She did not consider Indian dance a classical art form. She even called it fake and "folky", despite the fact that classical dance and theatre and music are written down in a treatise with all the rules and techniques, and never mind that the Indian civilisation is thousands of years older than the West.'

Despite putting her future in jeopardy, Gulati decided to complain.

'When I went to the Arts Council of England to complain, I was told that because I did not have anything tenable that there was nothing they could do, because my feelings were "untenable".

'I tried to talk about my experiences but had to complete the project despite the racism me and my classical Indian dancers were facing.'

The other thing we often forget about people of colour, in any profession, is the pressure you are under. It is not just from the family but your entire community and anyone who looks like you. Acting is not one of the preferred professions for south Asians in the UK. Even today, but less so, parents want their offspring to excel in the sciences. If you take the arts, then it had better be business or the law. Fortunately, British Asians who know that pressure are beginning to realise that our children should be allowed to choose their own path, and it is a growing minority who hang onto the past. Yet it does not make it any easier for those under intense scrutiny of societal pressures from all sides.

'I got my role in *Dinnerladies* in 1997,' Gulati recalled. 'It was my first major job in TV, and I was a newcomer to television but not necessarily to the performing arts.

'I was told by my peer group that my role was too stereotypical despite the fact that I was doing my very best to ensure that never happened.

'I didn't control the writing. My job was to deliver it to the best of my ability, while holding my own relationship to it authentically.

'I felt exhausted by the pressure of the job and by the expectations placed on me as the first person of colour in such a high-profile comedy.'

Journalists can also create problems because of the way they view and write about actors of colour.

'People forget that Maxine Peake started her career on this show, and yet every time she and I are mentioned in the same breath in the press, she is considered as one the main cast leads whilst I am always described as the newcomer and the inexperienced one.

'This is the media machine "colour washing" the narrative of my career.'

People of colour continue to complain about the idea that our feelings, our experiences, our perceptions cannot be real unless we can prove it beyond reasonable doubt in a court of law. And woe betide any actor or actress who decides to take the industry to court on the grounds of racism. What chances of a career then?

'I did an audition for a detective show playing at that time, as Asians were the victim of a crime, and it was in a post office,' Sanjeev Bhaskar recounted.

'Somebody in the post office had been coshed over the head and the police had come round.

'I went into the audition, having not really done auditions before, read the thing they wanted me to read, and it was one scene at the beginning when this detective comes in and says, "What happened, how many of them were there?"

'I read it, and the director said to me, "Could you maybe do it with an Indian accent?"'

What Bhaskar found, relatively early in his screen career, was that white cast directors wield power, and they are clear that they brook no nonsense from anyone, especially those who do not look like them.

'I said, "Oh I'm sorry, I didn't realise this character had just arrived from India."

'And he said, "Well he hasn't."

'I said "How old is he?" And he said, "Well he's about 34."

'"I'm 34," I said, "and my cousin runs a post office, and he doesn't have an Indian accent."

'And he said, "I don't think it sounds authentically Indian." And I said, "I've been Indian for 34 years, how long have you been Indian?"

'And then he showed me the door.'

Humour aside, it is a telling experience, which Shobna Gulati sympathises with.

'In my late forties, I was on my first commercial musical theatre job which involved an international tour,' she said.

'I was the only performer of colour, and the only other minorities were very junior staff working in technical areas of the production.

'Whilst they would speak to me about how they were being treated they weren't able to speak out about the micro-aggressions that they themselves were experiencing that was probably their choice given their status and age at that time.

'When I spoke up, I was labelled as the villain of the piece because whilst I was "famous", I was an outsider to this particular genre.'

The more Gulati picked up and pointed out the racist behaviour, the worse it got for her.

'The perpetrators, who were invariably white, could cry when I pointed out these behaviours and somehow, I would be seen as the aggressor.

'I was told I was making too much of it all up and it was just banter. When one of the other performers was put on a warning because of the behaviour that I saw, I was blamed by the others, for making the complaint.

'I believed they acted inappropriately and stand by it, but I became the subject of everyone's contempt.'

This transference of blame is nothing new, for it is those with the power who make the decisions, no matter how perverse they appear. Inevitably, in the end, Gulati was isolated.

'I often just went to my room, no one really wanted to be seen to be "on my side".

'It was a 13-month tour away from my home and family. I lost so much weight the costume that I was wearing had to be altered twice.

'I was traumatised and still am by the whole experience and made to feel I only got the job because of "fame" and the diversity tick box and not talent. No action was ever taken by the management against those who had gaslighted my experiences, and as the fallout continues it continues to affect my mental health and self-confidence.

'I was denied invites to socials, and I was told that I didn't fit in with them. Socials were often arranged without me, and I was deliberately left out.'

The big challenge for many actors of colour is to escape crude stereotypes and be given roles where they can show their real talents. For Pasha Bocarie, the actor who played Rakesh Kotecha in *Emmerdale*, this struggle characterised much of his early acting career.

'In the real world I had held so many different jobs to earn a living from being a bar tender, doorman, estate agent, model, musician, chauffeur, the list goes on,' he explains. 'But when it came to casting, the only criteria required from me was to portray an Asian stereotype.'

He started his career with Ken Loach in an arranged marriage storyline, but 15 years later he finally got a break landing a significant role in ITV's *Emmerdale*. He leapt at the opportunity but says he was never properly made to feel welcome.

'After three years of travelling 400 miles per week from London to Leeds, never missing a day or being late, putting in the performances, and giving everything to the show, I was starting to feel isolated and disliked by my peers,' he recalls. 'It's true such behaviour is part and parcel of any competitive process but it had become hostile. There were some very powerful actors in the cast, who had a lot of influence at every level. At award ceremonies or events I often found myself standing alone while the other white cast members congregated together ignoring me. I was made to feel that I had no right to be more prominent than them in the show as I was not English.'

The aloofness he experienced from other cast members was reflected in what he saw as a lack of recognition from the show's makers.

'Despite successive producers calling me in to their office and praising my performances and professionalism, my work was never publicly acknowledged,' he explains. 'I never received any nominations in three years from ITV, in contrast to the new white cast members who joined the show and within two weeks would get nominated. In fact, during my three years at Emmerdale, no minority actor was nominated for anything.'

He contrasts the strange and unwelcoming environment on set to the huge support he received from the show's audience.

'I received nothing but love and acceptance from a public who had embraced change and treated me as their own,' he says.

Another of our great south Asian talents is Meera Syal, who acts, writes and produces. An art polymath, who has been in the industry since the early 1980s, Syal is a pioneer who has faced her fair share of racism.

The problem, says Syal, is that it's always difficult to prove prejudice in the industry.

'The answer you will get from your agent is they've gone in a different direction, which actually could mean a million things. It could genuinely mean you're not right for the part, and that is part of being an actor, of course. Or does it mean, we don't think somebody with a brown face should play that part?

'But how are you ever going to prove that? So, it's really hard to pinpoint where that happens.'

What she can only point to is her experiences, despite being so well established and winning lots of awards.

'It's much clearer when I'm trying to get scripts off the ground, because most of the things I've written heavily feature south Asian characters, because that's what I'm interested in, and I feel we have so many untold stories that haven't been told before, then I do feel the quota system comes in.

'So many times have I heard, we have something similar, which doesn't mean we have something that is exactly the same idea as yours, it just means we have something with brown people in it, and we can't have both things at the same time.

'That makes me crazy mad.'

Speak to many in the profession who are of colour, and they tell you that they have had to go to America to win recognition. Syal gets that. The United States, she says, understands diversity. For the first time, the Disney Channel decided to commission a film where the central characters were south Asian. Called *Spin*, Syal said it went further than paying lip service to people of colour.

'It was just so great to be on a set where you weren't going, "Do you know what? We are actually a Hindu family, and that's a Muslim icon on the wall, that's a bit of the Quran, that might not work."

'There's a number of sets I've been on where that's happened. "No, no, actually, they're Sikhs and he wouldn't be called Iqbal Khan, sorry."

'I didn't have to do that because here was an Indian woman directing the film. So, it's not just about diversity in front of the camera, it's so important that we are represented behind the camera.

'In the crew, in the writing, the production, and in the direction, that's what makes the difference to authenticity.'

However, Syal said in her experience, diversity was always better in theatre than on screen, and it remained so.

'In theatre, I was being offered roles I would never ever play on screen, and still probably [would] not. A Peruvian millionaire in *Serious Money*, a deaf-mute girl in the seventeenth-century in *Birthright* at the Royal Court. In my first four or five years with the Royal Court, I did lots of parts that had nothing to do with race.'

What screen and television need to understand, argues Syal, is that they can effect change in society and the way the mainstream thinks.

'Before Obama was elected, there were three or four major films in which a black President was cast. At the time, people said, "Far-fetched, isn't it?" But then they did some research and directly linked those big blockbusters to the changing of people's attitudes and accepting a new kind of reality.

'They said the casting of these films actually helped Obama get elected, because suddenly people saw a reality that they thought could be possible.'

However, her partner, Sanjeev Bhaskar, still faces his fair share of rejections. You would have thought that with his high profile as an actor and his track record of writing award-winning comedic material, he would be much sought after by commissioners. Not so, he said.

'As a writer, it's much more difficult. On any project, there may be one writer and 100 actors. So, it's much more difficult.

'Somebody asked me this really interesting question when *Goodness Gracious Me* came out. It was Robert Elms on BBC Radio London and he said, "Do you hope that further down the line this won't be seen as Asian comedy, it will just be seen as comedy?"

'And I found myself saying, "No. I hope it doesn't." Because if it does then what makes us unique? This is British Asian comedy and if it's just comedy it's not specific anymore.

'I think carrying that into projects, either as an actor and particularly as a writer, helps you with this notion of specificity, when you're battling against, going back to my favourite topic, preconceptions and presumptions.'

Throughout my interview with Sanjeev, he typically sprinkled humour into serious thought. The point of his audition where he was asked to speak with an Indian accent illustrated one thing. Commissioners have their own idea of what 'Asian' means. Your idea, no matter how grounded it is in real life experience of actually being Asian, is useless because it may not accord with their perception through a white lens.

'It's slightly problematic because they are put into a position where they are weak,' Bhaskar continued. 'As a commissioner they want to be in a position where it's what they know, and they have control.

'We were lucky in *Goodness Gracious Me* in that once we were given the series, we were kind of left alone. That's why we were able to push the boat in so many directions.

'Subsequently whenever I take ideas in, this is something that's a bit of a battle.

'It's slightly easier now in the pre-conception bit because a number of people have broken through the glass ceiling just within the media.

'It's important wherever it happens. It isn't just about me, or comedy or Asians in the media. It's about how we are perceived generally.'

What *Goodness Gracious Me* and *The Kumars at No. 42* did, however, was to show the authentic side of south Asians – through the brown lens, if you will. These shows were written by people who got it because they had lived it. That authenticity did several things, including showing that people of colour were different from white consumers of comedy. What we must concede is that the likes of Bhaskar, Syal and Gulati have paved the way and made it easier for others to follow in their footsteps.

'What's very flattering is people of Asian heritage here who have cited *GGM* as a turning point,' admits Bhaskar.

'Whether it's people like Nish Kumar or Romesh Ranganathan or Riz Ahmed, these were all people who said I was quite young when *GGM* came on, and I suddenly thought it was possible, and those are the same people who are continuing to challenge those preconceptions.

'Riz being nominated for an Oscar, being in a *Star Wars* film, Nish being a political comedian and Romesh doing his kind of off the wall stuff, they've all done it under their own steam.

'I do think it's easier for them because I don't think Nish or Romesh were asked by anyone whether Asians were funny.'

Let us never forget that the bottom line in any business – and show business is just that – is money. Money talks, and those in the industry realise that real power comes from those with their hands on the levers of power.

'It is getting out of the quota system in your head and actually [stop] thinking that there's only room for one Asian show a year, one Asian star, one Asian drama, one Asian comedy and to take that label right off it and go "What's good?" and not to worry about who's not going to watch it, who is going to watch it,' Meera Syal argues.

'Audiences are much smarter than they give them credit for. Audiences will watch what's good and they don't really care what colour the people are that are in it. They really don't. They just want to watch good stuff.'

Syal coined it as 'lazy racism'.

'We've just got to have really honest conversations, and I think that's happening,' she says.

'The change really will come when the people that hold the purse strings and the power are diverse, and the boardrooms are diverse, when the commissioners are diverse. It's not [at the moment].

'People think diversity is a headcount and you switch on your television and go, well there's one and there's one, I mean, they're all over the place, they're even in adverts now for God's sake. But that's actually quite superficial headcounts.'

The industry is in flux. In June 2020, more than 2,800 actors, producers, writers and production staff wrote an open letter to industry bosses urging them 'to tackle structural and systemic racism in our industry, in the UK'. That open letter was hard-hitting, brave, and demonstrated the decades of frustration endured by generations of professionals ignored by the white establishment.

'Banish "it's too small" from your lexicon. It is insulting to our stories, our history, our impact on world culture, and our worth,' the authors wrote.

'Our stories are referred to as "too small" because they do not centre around white characters or a small subset of actors whom you deem valuable; they are not always written by the same white writers that you deem to be "safe".

'Banish "we already have a diverse project on our slate". There is room for more than one.

'You make countless projects with similar themes and storylines with white creatives. Banish "that feels risky".'

And here is the killer point.

'We know we are introducing you to new unproven talent, but why is the same white man (*who has made a string of flops after his one hit 10 years ago*) still deemed less risky than a new brown or black writer with original and well written ideas?'

They have a point. For Shobna Gulati, the solution is surprisingly simple.

'Unless you set proper targets, using writers, makers, producers from different cultural backgrounds, we will make no progress,' she explains. 'Unless we set inclusive, representative meaningful targets we will make no proper progress.'

She wants the industry's decision-makers to walk a mile in her shoes, and that of anyone who happens not to fit the male, pale, stale trope.

'There are so many narratives, and these voices and people don't necessarily have to be new or young.

'There are so many who didn't get the opportunity and despite this still soldier on. Let them bring their experience and story to the table, too.

'There has to be a space where stories and representation are on an equal playing field, where the opportunity of access is open, where competition for the slot is equal.

'There should be more than one slot. I know of actors with dual heritage who don't fit any particular racial profile. Many of them are exhausted with trying to fit into casting and are coming away from the profession.'

That is one major problem when it comes to the media. The industry sticks with the tried and tested, no matter how much they flop – as long as they are white. Why else would so many of our ethnic stars seek their fortunes in Hollywood? Sure, the industry is bigger. But there must be a simpler explanation. Could it be that what has happened in America is that black women, and it is mainly black women, have decided to take financial risks and show Hollywood that the only colour that matters is green?

The most well-known is Oprah Winfrey. *Forbes* puts her wealth in 2021 at $2.6 billion, describing her as 'entrepreneur, personality, philanthropist'. 'Producer, screenwriter, author' Shonda Rhimes, *Forbes* said, was worth about $150 million. In 2017, the producer of hit shows where black women are the lead characters, such as *Scandal*, signed a five-year deal with Netflix.

However, Syal correctly pointed out that Britain could have been ahead of the curve.

'If you want to get a script onto British television, there is probably only about six people that have the power to commission. That is a tiny, tiny little bubble. In America, it's the land of immigrants, and they have a completely different view of diverse casting anyway, and the industry is much bigger.

'It's very sad. There's been a real brain drain; one of the things that makes me really sad actually is particularly south Asian female representation. If I think about *Bhaji on the Beach*, it was way ahead of anything that America has done. If I think that *Goodness Gracious Me* happened way before anything America's ever done.

'It feels like we started it here, but then the Americans took the baton and ran right past us, because they were willing to go, "We want some new, diverse voices, and we don't see you in a specific box, so here we are, what stories do you want to tell?" That's not happening here.'

This does show a staggering myopia and missed opportunity.

'When the boardrooms change, when the people who sit in the seats of power are actually diverse in their head and their heart, then we won't have to have these conversations, we won't have to keep explaining ourselves,' adds Syal.

Like Gulati, Sanjeev Bhaskar knows that it is the minority who spoil it for the majority.

'From my experience I don't think Britain was ever a racist country,' he says. 'It was always the vocal minority that pushed it. I think perceptions have changed.

'The idea of who we were as south Asians or what black people are, are very, very different in 2021 to what they were in 1971. The landscape has changed and for most people of 14, 15, when it comes to things like attitudes towards women, the #MeToo movement, diversity [they have changed].

'I've never limited diversity to skin colour. In Britain it's also about gender and Scotland, Wales, Northern Ireland as well, because until we see those as our stories, there will always be an "other".'

'The "other" will always exist. Everything I've tried to do is make that definition of the "other" as narrow as I possibly can.'

Bhaskar's optimism does not mean we can afford to be complacent. Far from it. But in the past few years, on-screen representation has changed beyond recognition. That change has been hard fought. That change is because streaming services, like Netflix, get that diversity sells. *Bridgerton*, produced by Shonda Rhimes, is a key example, forcing the more established BBC and ITV to realise that they face losing generations if they do not change.

But the danger is that change is superficial. Take the 2021 ITV series *Darling Buds of May*. Charlie is now black, and the 1950s' village has two south Asians, one of whom has a thick Indian accent, and the other is a British Army veteran. While this appears great on the surface, they retain the same stereotypical and racist tropes of the 1970s. That same old argument: how people of colour are, how we are expected to behave, through a white-person's lens.

The levers of power come with a meaningful budget and the ability to make meaningful decisions. Until we realise that, until we act rather than talk, until we put a critical mass of people in those positions, nothing will truly change.

5

EDUCATION

Ending a culture of denial

Universities have always been at the forefront of attempts to protect human rights. From student protests in the 1960s, to the anti-fascism rallies that I took part in during the 1980s, activism has been ever present on university campuses throughout history.

Universities had a key part to play in the civil rights movement in the United States, for example, and the campus battles that took place fighting against the war in Vietnam and standing up for fairness and equality were hugely influential. We think of universities as hubs of liberal academic freedom where who you are doesn't matter but what you think does.

It should therefore come as a surprise to learn that these institutions which are challenging inequality in society are not exactly embracing a model of inclusivity themselves and are badly lacking diversity in their senior leadership. As I write, there are only three Vice Chancellors from minority communities out of over 130 universities in this country, and the situation in relation to deputies and assistants is just as bad.

Add to that the poverty of minority representation in the governing bodies and you have an obvious crisis in confidence. I was a Governor and then Pro-Chancellor at Brunel University in west London and have been privileged to be awarded four honorary doctorates by British institutions. It's quite telling that the institutions that have honoured me are some of the most diverse in this country and that their award is meant to be a recognition of the journey that they have been on and my commitment to it.

That symbolism, however, does little to address what can only be described as a chronic lack of black and Asian minority ethnic representation at the top.

This crisis has inevitably led to accusations of prejudice from commentators in the media, as well as searing criticism from within the academies themselves, highlighting the daily plight of black and Asian staff and the impenetrable glass ceiling that they're up against.

It certainly begs the question as to whether these institutions, known the world over for their culture of challenging injustice and promoting equality of opportunity, have a problem with racism. Could this explain the lack of diversity in top jobs?

According to Professor David Richardson, Vice Chancellor at the University of East Anglia, it most certainly does, and demonstrates deep structural unfairness that has been ignored for too long.

Speaking in BBC Three's 2021 documentary, *Is Uni Racist?*, Professor Richardson argued, 'There is a lot of evidence that points towards universities perpetuating systemic racism, being institutionally racist'.

The programme, presented by journalist Linda Adey, investigated the experiences of four black students at British universities. In it, Richardson highlighted systemic issues that disproportionately affect black and minority ethnic students.

In case you were wondering, Professor Richardson is a white man. He is also Chair of Universities UK Advisory Group to tackle racial harassment in higher education.

The question of whether or not the programme makers attempted to interview a black Vice Chancellor is, well, academic, as when the documentary was being made, they would not have found one at any UK university.

The first and to date only black Vice Chancellor, Professor Charles Egbu, was appointed by Leeds Trinity University and assumed duties on 1 November 2020, just a few months before the programme aired.

And, when it comes to university top jobs, the role of Vice Chancellor is not the only one where black people are gravely underrepresented.

Statistics published by the Higher Education Statistics Agency for the academic year 2020/21 showed that just 160 out of 22,855 professors were black. That is fewer than 1 per cent, despite the fact that we have some of the most culturally diverse student intakes in Europe. In some universities, over 50 per cent of students come from BAME backgrounds.

In February 2022, one of the few mainstream media outlets reporting on these statistics, the *i* newspaper, ran the following headline: 'Empowering Black People to Become Academics "Should be Top Priority" as Data Reveals Poor Diversity Levels'.

Their report quotes Andrea E.L. Attipoe, bioengineering PhD student and a member of ICL Black Doctoral Network, at Imperial College, who said the figures were 'appalling'. This lack of representation, she said, 'results in a lack of role models at every stage of academia, which further discourages students to evolve in an environment sometimes perceived as rejecting and hostile.'

Several other people interviewed for the article added that they'd never encountered or been taught by a black academic during the course of their studies. Sofia Akel, Race, Education and Black

Studies Lecturer, said these figures confirmed a worrying trend. 'To be disappointed is to have expected more from the sector,' she said. 'Higher education is an institution that sustains and thrives off institutional racism.'

This underrepresentation at the top is not just confined to universities when it comes to the education sector, nor does it affect black people in isolation.

There is clear evidence that all minorities of black and Asian ethnicity are underrepresented in senior roles in all UK educational institutions, including schools and colleges. In England, for example, only 7.3 per cent of headteachers in state-funded schools come from minority-ethnic backgrounds, despite making up 21.5 per cent of the working-age population.

Does this lack of diversity in senior roles, taken together with the findings of the documentary, and the evidence that Professor Richardson alludes to, necessarily mean that universities, and educational establishments more generally, have a deep-rooted problem with diversity at leadership level? And, if so, how might this impact upon the progression of minority ethnic staff working within these institutions?

To find out more, I spoke to a number of senior staff from minority ethnic backgrounds working in the education sector. Unsurprisingly, most chose to remain anonymous.

One who didn't was Professor Zahir Irani.

I first met Zahir in 2013 at Brunel University London, where he was Head of Brunel Business School. At this time, he was leading one of the most successful business schools in the country, though this hadn't always been the case. He had taken the school from being under, in effect, special measures in 2006 when his tenure began, to one that went on to win the *Times Higher Education* Awards Business School of the Year in 2013.

I wanted to catch up with him to find out about his experiences while he was at Brunel. In particular, I wanted to understand how he felt he had been treated based specifically on his minority ethnic status during his time there.

My personal recollection of the Brunel University board was that it was extremely diverse. In fact, I remember that around half of the board and senior management team were from minorities – though not the Vice Chancellor.

Zahir shares a similar view, but notes that the situation changed for him in late 2013, after there appeared to be 'no more roles' for him.

Subsequently, he went off to do a 12-month secondment at the Cabinet Office, acting as Senior Policy Advisor. On his return, Zahir learned that his previous role had 'expired', so he applied to become one of the three Deans that had recently been created in a restructured senior management team. He was successful, and was appointed Founding Dean of College (Business, Arts, Social Sciences).

He observed at this time that the diversity on the board and representation in the senior leadership team had diminished during the short time he'd been away. Across the sector, he saw representation falling. 'Universities should be pioneers in increasing diversity, but the opposite was happening,' he recalls.

I personally recall that there seemed to be no conversation or understanding about what was happening or what had happened at this time. There was certainly no discussion at University Council about relinquishing a commitment to diversity. I remember, as Zahir does, that any discussion on this subject was initiated by people from minorities and, if they hadn't initiated the conversations, it wouldn't have been discussed.

Zahir is currently Deputy Vice Chancellor at the University of Bradford. Here, he tells me, equality and diversity are embedded in the community and there is great affection and goodwill among the people of Bradford towards the university. He says that, in contrast to Brunel, here he is 'supported in discussions about equality and diversity, particularly by the Vice Chancellor, who clearly feels that social inclusion is a priority'.

There have been occasions, he jokes, where he has not been charged for restaurant meals because of the goodwill that the city has for its university. Bradford itself is an extraordinarily diverse city, though we may discuss the diversity of the city's senior leadership on another occasion.

Zahir told me about his application to become Vice Chancellor at City University in London. He accepts that the person who was appointed was fully deserving of it. He does, however, reflect upon the process. As part of this, he met with half of the main board in what was a very challenging interview. Between the interviews, one of the board members approached Bradford University after this interview about some of the answers that he had given. This was an attempt to undermine the credibility of his answers and demonstrated a lack of trust in what he had said. When Zahir became aware and mentioned this to the head hunters, they too were aghast. Why would this be necessary? They refused to accept his answers without verifying them themselves. Would they have done that had he been white? To add insult to injury, at his final interview one of the panel members came out in order to bring in the next candidate and asked Zahir if he could turn down the air-conditioning unit. The panel member had assumed that the brown person in the suit was not Vice Chancellor material, this despite the fact that Zahir's picture is plastered on his CV.

Of course when you approach Universities UK and other organisations which purportedly represent university management, they make reference to the guidelines which include having an individual from minorities at the final stage of interview processes for their senior leaders. I've seen this before and it's perceived as nothing more than box ticking. It's also supposedly an insurance policy against criticism for being biased, were someone to question the fairness of the selection. It makes it even more difficult to be able to prove that the process was not fair and they have deliberately interviewed a person from a minority, but not appointed them.

Despite these guidelines, there's a widely held view that institutions decide who they want as CEO or another leadership position and work backwards to devise a 'transparent process of selection' which delivers the outcome and the person they want. One problem with this approach is that there is no more than a nod to diversifying the leadership cadre whilst a board merely selects a leader they want who maintains the status quo in terms of diversity – that is, not enough of it.

A mainly white or exclusively white board selects a white leader despite there being several appointable people of colour that could do the job. Worse, they devise a process that ensures at least one non-white applicant is shortlisted and select an interview panel which contains at least one non-white panel member. Why do I say that's worse? Because plenty of people told me that it makes the selection 'employment tribunal proof', unchallengeable as, prima facie, the selection was non-discriminatory. The non-white panel member is rarely, if ever, the Chair or Deputy Chair so is railroaded to support the choice of candidate. The non-white shortlisted candidate is a vaccine against criticism that they never seriously considered a more diverse selection.

That being said, it's increasingly more difficult to prove than the outright racism that, for example, my black colleagues and I experienced at the hands of a white only civil service selection panel in the late 1990s. That was upheld by a tribunal largely because the panel Chair was so sure they would get away with it, that he wrote things on his panel marking sheets which showed his prejudices. These days, they aren't going to do that, unless they're really stupid. It's much more sophisticated.

Now, let me present some facts and you can draw your own conclusion.

Aston University in Birmingham is an excellent seat of learning which often gets overlooked because of its bigger cousin, Birmingham University, where I did my undergraduate degree. Aston, in fact, was awarded 'University of the Year' by the *Guardian* in 2020. It was led by an inspiring leader, Professor Alec Cameron. He decided to quit at the end of 2021 and take up a new position of Vice Chancellor in Australia at RMIT University in Melbourne. Not surprising, as most of his career was down under.

His replacement at Aston is Professor Aleks Subic, who started in the summer of 2022. His previous posting was Deputy Vice Chancellor at RMIT University in Australia. That's a little bit surprising because it sounds very much to many at the university as a quasi job-swap. Not entirely, of course, because a Deputy became the Vice Chancellor of a university who had left to become Vice Chancellor of the university where the Deputy worked. Still, of all the leaders in all of international academia, it's quite a coincidence.

Nobody has suggested that there was anything improper in the appointment.

Were there any non-white candidates from the UK that might have filled one of the small number of Vice Chancellor appointments that come up each year? Did we have to bring in another white leader from abroad? In fact, as I understand it, to get a work visa there must be no other appointable candidates from within the UK. Some within the university told me that there was at least one non-white candidate in the UK who was deemed to be 'appointable'. Still, they chose someone who looks like their outgoing leader and, in fact, came from where their former leader is now leading!

All of it, of course, can be explained without resorting to allegations of racism or nepotism.

My point is that our most liberal institutions need to lead by example. Yet they lag far behind the private sector in appointing more diverse leaders. It seems easier for them to appoint people who look like them, giving people of colour little chance of advancement.

Our most highly regarded institutions are the so called Russell Group – institutions such as the one I went to at Birmingham, for example. They're not your Oxford or Cambridge but they are seen as good predictors of future employment prospects. Again, it appears that in order to become Vice Chancellor of a Russell Group university, you will need to be a senior member in a Russell Group university. So somebody like Zahir would have to take a step down from his deputy Vice Chancellor role in order to get into a relatively less senior role at a Russell Group university before, he believes, he would be considered for a Deputy or Vice Chancellor role there. It appears therefore to be a 'reserved role'. If you're not part of the group then you have a lot less chance of progressing.

When I began examining diversity at leadership level in universities, I expected to discover that the majority fully embraced the need for this and were leading the way on issues of equality; tackling underrepresentation at every turn; setting an example for other institutions to follow.

What I found out, however, was that Bradford's commitment to equality and diversity would be the exception, rather than the rule.

According to most of the people I spoke to, structural racism is still a major barrier to promotion at UK universities, and many of the people I interviewed for this chapter found it painful to talk about their experiences.

One woman, who shared her experiences as a Senior Lecturer at a major UK university in the north of England, began by telling me about blatant examples of overt racism that she witnessed from colleagues.

'Within my department, I have heard senior managers use the "n" word in telling stories, in some instances, as if they were saying something slightly risqué, so long as no one else overheard – perhaps the fact that I am a person of colour absolved them a little; an underhand version of "them and us".

'I remember every single time a person has used a racist term, phrase, or trope to insult me, or when it has been used in passing to demean another person. It's exhausting.'

It's the first time she has ever spoken openly about how a culture of racism in the workplace has affected her and the barriers to promotion she's faced. It's not something she finds easy, not least because on the rare occasions that she has expressed concerns to her employers about feeling uncomfortable, she has been met with thinly veiled suggestions that she is 'pulling out the race card'.

The unpalatable truth, she said, is that 'I must tolerate racism in my workplace because it is part of the culture, and I can't change that.'

Like many others, she felt her only option was to work hard, swimming against a tide of stereotypes and prejudice, to achieve small successes.

Those successes, by the way, are not so 'small'. She is an award-winning researcher who publishes in high-impact peer-reviewed academic journals and presents her work at academic and professional conferences to international audiences.

Her successes are not limited to research either. In fact, the degree course she leads is consistently the most popular within the school in terms of student numbers. She also sits on numerous panels and takes an active role in shaping university policy.

This impressive track record of achievement extends beyond academia, too. Her work informs local and national Government policy, and she leads a well-known global network of academics and practitioners.

I asked her if she feels that the university, which is the ultimate beneficiary of her achievements and the esteem they bring, has sufficiently rewarded her in terms of promotion.

'I have seen recently qualified colleagues, with far fewer credentials, promoted to senior leadership roles ahead of me,' she says. 'The criteria for numerous promotions that I have been passed over in favour of a white person, not only have I met, I have exceeded.

'There is little effort made to disguise this bias,' she says. 'My manager once tied himself up in knots trying to explain why a person, who had qualified just a couple of years earlier, and had only three publications (one of which I helped them write), had been promoted ahead of me.'

He had told her that, in order for her to progress, she needed grant capture. She adds, with a wry smile, that she had been Principal Investigator on two successful grant applications within the past two years and is able to demonstrate a sustained track record of developing proposals to secure external grants.

'When I pointed this out to him,' she says, 'he basically moved the goal posts by telling me that I needed "more" grant capture.'

Funding, incidentally, is a lesser known barrier that ethnic minority academics face to progression. Over the past 10 years or so grant capture has become an increasingly important factor in successful applications for promotion.

However, analysis from UK data reveals that academics from ethnic minorities are less likely to get funding than white people. Principal Investigators who are white win grant proposals 27 per cent of the time compared with 17 per cent of the time for ethnic minorities.

Might this discrepancy, I ask her, be accounted for when universities set targets for successful applications?

'It would certainly go some small way to levelling the playing field,' she says.

Moving on to the issue of underrepresentation of black and Asian people at senior levels in academia, I ask her about the effects this situation has had on her ambitions.

'I am about to turn 50,' she says, 'and throughout my career as a research academic, I have worked in a predominately white middle-class discipline and environment. I have witnessed and experienced first hand many of the biases and barriers that students and staff from minority backgrounds face.

'Since starting my undergraduate degree 25 years ago, until now, in my current role as Senior Lecturer I have been, with only two exceptions, the only south Asian student on my course or staff member in my department. During this period, I have not had one student peer or academic colleague of black heritage.'

The experience has been chronically demotivating, she argues.

'The lack of representative role models and mentors has, throughout my academic career, had a profound negative effect on my ambitions. It wasn't until approximately five years ago that I felt really capable of progressing.'

I asked her about what had happened five years ago that caused her to find her confidence.

'The honest answer,' says, laughing, 'is my husband, who is a white man! From him, and the friends and allies I've sought outside of the university, I draw the courage to confront rather than shy away from the problem of racism at work. When I find myself in doubt, I talk to the people who understand.'

Without allies and a strong support base, she admits that she'd feel even more isolated.

'It often feels like an uphill battle,' she says before we end the interview, 'and it's one that I shouldn't have to fight at all. It is as though universities are blind to the fact that, in supporting the progression of black and Asian staff, they improve the experience of students. Who are, after all, their bread and butter.'

Another person I spoke to, who also wished to remain anonymous, related to me their experience of applying for a Principal position at a college in the Midlands.

He had held a Vice Principal post at another college for a couple of years and then decided to 'test the waters' in terms of progression.

The interview was in a relatively small college in a small town. After his first interview, he tells me, 'I withdrew my application since I did not see this as a sufficiently challenging role.'

But this wasn't the end of it, he says. After about two weeks, I was surprised to receive a letter from the Race Equality Commission informing me that a Governor and member of the interview panel had lodged a complaint that when the panel were making their decision regarding who should be offered the post of Principal at the College, certain members of the panel, they alleged, made discriminating remarks about my candidature.

'I was asked about my opinion regarding the possibility of a formal investigation. My response was that I was unable to comment on "what went on behind closed doors" but if a formal complaint was made, then the Commission should proceed with their enquiry and keep me informed.'

When the Commission for Racial Equality eventually published its report, he tells me, 'They sent me additional details of what took place in the final selection process for the post of Principal, much of which was not published in the final report.'

According to this secondary report, all Council Officers and three of the Governors favoured his appointment, and just two of the Governors favoured the internal candidate. During deliberations, the two Governors who were in favour of the internal candidate asked the Governor, who was also the Chair of the panel, to withdraw from the room to have a private discussion – in contravention of the normal interview process. When the panel reconvened, the Chair changed her mind, with no explanation, and used her casting vote in favour of the internal candidate.

Elaborating on the content of this secondary report, he said, 'It is interesting to note that during the Commission's investigation, the Chair's affidavit said, "Candidate B (me) also interviewed well but tended to talk about educational concepts during his interview, rather than the practicalities of the job".'

The Commission found this statement contradicted the Governor's interview record. Under the heading of 'Application', she had written: 'Excellent, clear grasp of what is expected of a Principal and the future development of a College.' She also noted: 'Good experience of curriculum work and the importance of entitlement curriculum.' Under Staff Development, she wrote: 'Strong and practical interest in staff development and appraisal.' Various other positive feedback was included in the detailed records.

He explains that, 'With this evidence, the Commission found that the Chair of the panel was not telling the truth about my performance at interview and they concluded that the true reason for not appointing me was that I was Asian.'

As well as this unfortunate episode, the Commission reported that when shortlisting for the Principal's post, a Governor also objected to the appointment of an Asian.

'Since I withdrew from the interview process for this post after the first day, the Governor's objection did not apply,' he admits. 'These two instances clearly indicated that whilst the majority of Governors were open minded and objective in their work as college Governors, there was a minority with deep-rooted prejudice.'

Uncovering this clear bias had the negative effect of putting him off from applying for the post of Principal for a number of years.

When he did eventually decide to apply, he says 'there were occasions when I felt that my interview performance was very poor, and I would find it difficult to appoint myself to the posts.'

There have, he tells me, been several other occasions since, where he suspected that an element of discrimination had taken place.

In one incident, in which the recruitment was carried out by a reputable national company, he had phoned to get an update on the progress of his application before going on a short vacation. He was told by a manager at the company that he was one of the top three applicants they would be recommending to the Governors for interview and appointment.

On his return, he contacted the company to seek further information regarding his application. The same manager informed him that, despite their recommendation, the Governors did not wish to include him on the shortlist for interview because they felt he 'would not fit in'.

He was unable to pursue this further since he could not gather any further information from the company responsible for the recruitment process.

In another example of possible discrimination, in which he progressed with two other candidates to the final selection process, the two senior local authority officers present at interview suggested that he was the 'best candidate' for the post. The Governors, however, decided to appoint the internal 'white' candidate.

In this particular situation, he says, 'To the best of my knowledge, no formal complaints were made and the local authority officer who informed me of the outcome did not wish to pursue this further.'

As our conversation draws to a close, and with a bittersweet sigh, he tells me that 'after less than two years into the post, following a very poor inspection report, the appointee was dismissed.'

Hearing about these experiences of bias in the education sector, it was easy to understand why the people I was speaking to wished to remain anonymous. For example, another person I spoke to told me about her experiences of discrimination while working in further education.

While employed as a senior manager in a southwest England college, the Principal (a white man) had left suddenly for another job. As the senior manager in charge of the majority of the college, she considered applying for the now vacant Principal role.

Her hopes were dashed, however, when the Chair (a white woman) told her, in no uncertain terms, that she would not be considered. The college went on to appoint a younger white man with less experience and fewer skills than her because, she suspects, 'he was known to the Chair through her governance roles'.

She goes on to describe many examples of the micro-aggressions that she suffered, along with incidents of overt racism where people would ask her, 'Where are you really from?' or 'Where are your parents from?' On top of which there were regular comments about the way she looked, and her dress and hair. She never heard such comments directed at her white female CEO counterparts.

'People see my success despite racism and therefore feel they can say racism didn't affect me. I know different. It took me a long time to find my voice,' she says.

Most of the people I spoke to in the higher education sector were happy to confirm that universities were far from inclusive and were in denial about a discriminatory culture. This manifested itself in incidents of overt racism, being ignored and other micro-aggressions, being mistaken for the cleaner, or being warned off applying for senior posts because they 'wouldn't fit in'.

They expressed concerns about reporting any of this and the barriers they face. Most feared their complaints would be dismissed and they would be singled out as a troublemaker, who couldn't be trusted.

Many similar experiences and concerns were relayed in a 2019 report published by the Equality and Human Rights Commission (EHRC), called *Tackling Racial Harassment: Universities Challenged.* Based on the results of an EHRC inquiry into racial harassment in publicly funded universities in Britain, it examined staff and students' experiences of racial harassment and the effect that this might have on their education, career and wellbeing.

According to the inquiry, over half of staff who responded to the survey described incidents of being ignored or excluded because of their race. And more than a quarter said they experienced racist name-calling, insults and jokes.

Yet, despite this widespread prevalence of racism, the survey found that fewer than half of all staff who had experienced racial harassment reported it to their university.

One of the reasons given for this failure to report was because they feared the personal consequences that reporting might have on their education, career and wellbeing, or worried they would not be supported, and ostracised as a result.

A pattern has emerged in this sector over recent years of staff experiencing racism in silence because the only alternative is to risk jeopardising their promotion prospects. And, given what we now know, this fear of reporting abuse and prejudiced behaviour is entirely rational.

Might this underreporting go some way to explaining the seemingly low priority given to tackling racism in UK universities? If the many troubling incidents I heard aren't being reported, then how can university administrators know that they have a problem?

The answer is that they do know they have a problem. They also know that they have an incomplete picture of the scale of the problem and that underreporting is one of the reasons for this.

But, instead of addressing the issue of underreporting so that they can get the fullest picture, universities routinely fail to record informal complaints. In cases where they do record complaints, the EHRC found that just one in six staff complaints of racial harassment were upheld. Is it any wonder that ethnic minority staff don't go to the trouble?

Universities have access to the same data that I researched for this book, and a good deal of non-public internal data besides. The real question isn't about whether or not they know they have a problem with institutional racism; it is about the appetite shown to ignore it or, at the very least, to downplay the scale of it.

Presumably, for most administrators, accepting that their university suffers from institutional racism must be their worst public relations nightmare – which may go some way to explaining why it's continually hidden.

The EHRC report lends this hypothesis some weight. They found that there was a strong perception that universities too often place their reputation above the safeguarding and welfare of their staff and students.

The report quotes staff and students who said that policies and leadership commitments to tackling racism were 'often undermined by a lack of meaningful enforcement'.

It could well have added an insufficiently strong or brave model of leadership. Because in order to tackle the very real and current problem of racism and prejudice, universities will first need to acknowledge that the problem exists. This will take courage and leadership. And, inevitably, it will mean that the public will find out about it.

For most leaders this will be a step too far. Weighing up reputational management and the likely impact that a racism scandal might have on recruiting the best talent and attracting the student numbers they need to meet revenue targets will almost certainly tip the scales in one direction. This will mean they play down incidents and refuse to grasp the nettle.

However, they should draw courage from examples where universities have acknowledged a problem and been proactive in addressing it rather than playing it down. These show that universities can enhance their reputation by promoting safeguarding policies and strategies to prospective and existing staff and students.

A good example is Durham University's decision not to shy away from the scandal of rape and sexual assault on their campus, which was exposed by national media. Rather than try to avoid the issue, they went out of their way to address people's concerns during an open day for prospective students and their parents. This acknowledgement by the university, and details about their efforts to address the problem, resulted in a significant rise in applicant numbers.

Whether or not universities are ready to take this first step and acknowledge they have a race problem is not clear. Neither are there signs of any real enthusiasm to start removing a toxic culture and replace it with one that genuinely values diversity and moves to conscious inclusion.

As Professor David Richardson noted in a 2021 Universities UK media release: 'It is my firm belief that UK universities perpetuate institutional racism. This is uncomfortable to acknowledge but all university leaders should do so as a first step towards meaningful change.'

Universities must become places where racism is not tolerated and where problems with racism and racial discrimination are discussed competently and constructively. They must create a culture where staff and students are able to work and learn in a safe and welcoming environment, where progression is not dependent on the colour of their skin.

This certainly isn't going to be easy.

To quote a 2016 *Guardian* article by academic and author Professor Kehinde Andrews: 'doing so means recognising our privilege; the regressive role that universities continue to play in society, and the institutional barriers we must overcome'.

The level of change needed is going to require that those people at the top levels of university decision-making are fully engaged in solving the problem.

Throwing small pots of cash at diversity training and anti-bias training may be the current go-to solutions for most university administrators. But this is not working – these short-term interventions rarely change people, never really win hearts and minds, and are little more than a sticking plaster.

Vice Chancellor groups and university management teams need to put the problems of racism, exclusion and prejudice on the top of their to-do lists. It needs to be a priority. And then they need to start looking at the data on hiring, retention, promotion and pay to identify what's gone wrong and to seek solutions.

Getting to grips with and understanding the contours of the problem will require significant engagement with people from different ethnic groups who wish to progress. It will mean university leaders embedding a culture where everyone becomes a champion of diversity, not just a few token diversity ambassadors in HR. New structures will need to be put in place along with mentorship programmes, which universities desperately lack. And above all, it will require the use of one of the most important skills known to mankind.

That of active listening.

6

ENTERPRISE

'Moving away from business as usual'

State Street is one of the largest investment firms in the world and also one of the oldest financial institutions in America. Its history can be dated back to the founding years of Boston's banking industry and for centuries it has been at the heart of a financial industry that has suffered from snowy peaks syndrome, where the top positions are nearly always held by white people.

It's not just in the United States where those snowy peaks remain stubbornly uniform and closed to ethnic minority talent, though. With industry surveys showing that ethnic minority finance workers in London have not only suffered racial discrimination, but believe it's holding back their careers, it's hardly surprising that the UK's financial watchdog is poised to publish requirements to introduce targets to boost diversity.

But, while many banks and financial institutions have remained silent about their diversity problem, State Street, who have offices in Canary Wharf and are very much part of our financial landscape, have been actively turning up the volume for several years.

In 2016 they introduced an investment fund devoted to gender diverse companies, and then, the following year, they unveiled Fearless Girl, a bronze statue of a young girl staring down the famous Wall Street charging bull outside the New York Stock Exchange. It came to symbolise economic empowerment for women and was hailed as a cultural turning point.

They have subsequently used their investment arm to vote against directors of big companies that fail to disclose the racial and ethnic makeup of their boards, before announcing a bold plan to triple the number of female and ethnic minority staff in senior roles by 2023.

Then the backlash started.

'No Country for White Men as State Street Push Diversity', screamed one newspaper headline. Reports went on to claim that staff would have to get 'special approval to hire a white man, rather than a woman or an ethnic-minority candidate'.

Naturally this didn't land well with some people and when Fox News picked up on the story staff began to get abused.

'The story wasn't even true but I've had angry calls at three in the morning from people yelling at me that I'm evil,' explains their global Head of PR, Sarah Higgins. 'They say we are denying their sons and daughters jobs and that we're the lowest of the low. It's toxic. Everyone has been on the receiving end of abuse.'

Higgins concedes they are currently some way off this target and says I am the first person to contact the company with a positive interest in their diversity goals.

The frustration and disappointment in her voice is a timely reminder that changing centuries-old power structures is always going to be extremely hard and will be resisted by many who feel threatened.

But it also demonstrates that those companies who wish to open up leadership positions to new talent cannot achieve greater diversity simply through well-meaning announcements or ambitious targets.

State Street is not the only company to embrace diversity targets. While businesses across multiple sectors are now talking openly about ramping up diversity efforts, this does not always translate into more inclusive businesses. Frequently, businesses are adopting a tokenistic approach to appointments, which gives the appearance of culture change when what is happening is little more than window dressing. It creates resentment, and economists have warned that taking an 'add diversity and stir' approach, while business continues as normal will not change anything. To really embrace diversity, business needs to change its culture.

Certainly the Diversity, Equity and Inclusion agenda is fast becoming something businesses can no longer ignore. Yet, while it's championed everywhere from Davos to the UN, many are still struggling with deep-seated problems.

Research conducted by Henley Business School in 2020 found that 30 per cent of business leaders and almost a quarter (24 per cent) of employees felt that racial inequity exists in their organisation, with that figure rising to as many as two in five (40 per cent) of employees from ethnic minorities and one in three (37 per cent) business leaders from minority backgrounds. There were also generational differences in the data. The research found that younger white employees (29 per cent of 18–34-year-olds) and younger white business leaders (41 per cent of 18–34-year-olds) are more likely to acknowledge that inequity exists than older white employees (15 per cent of +55-year-olds) and older white business leaders (15 per cent of +55-year-olds). Ethnic minority female business leaders are also more likely than their male counterparts to acknowledge that inequity exists in their business (44 per cent versus 31 per cent).

There are also differentials based on size and type of company, but the leadership of a company is critical in determining the extent to which inclusive values, processes and practices are embedded. Furthermore, we need to be aware of the lack of diversity across functions, which may in turn lead to a narrow path through to executive roles. Green Park's annual FTSE 100 Business Leaders Index, for example, highlights that Britain's female and ethnic minority business leaders are largely found in areas of the business such as HR, Diversity, and Marketing & Communications. They hold less influence, have lower salaries and are less likely to be on track to C-Suite (top senior executive) roles. Their survey also revealed that one of the least diverse functions within UK companies is Diversity & Inclusion, which is disproportionately a white and female preserve – nearly two out of three of these senior roles are filled by white women.

There are enduring structures to be found in some UK businesses that disadvantage people from different ethnic communities. But there are also cultural dimensions that leave some people with a sense of alienation, marginalisation and a feeling of not being fully accepted or valued. From my conversations with business leaders from different ethnic backgrounds, it is clear that a feeling of not belonging is very much a common sentiment, which has resulted in them adopting a range of coping mechanisms. The context of the pandemic has been an interesting one, with some feeling more marginalised than ever before, while others have seen the move to remote working to be something of a leveller. Working from home obviously reduced the social connectivity and dynamics that can be a forum for 'banter', where some have felt targeted, particularly through micro-aggressions. The post-pandemic working environment will, once again, create challenges for some as they gradually return to an office setting. Unfortunately, it is sometimes this very setting, where some see an 'in crowd' of those whose voices are heard and those who have access to the promotion pipeline versus those who remain on the margins and feel they have to work twice as hard as their white counterparts.

In challenging times, anything that is not deemed essential can be de-prioritised. During the financial crisis of 2008, women and, more broadly, people from different ethnic backgrounds were disproportionately affected. Once again, we find ourselves in that category of 'challenging times' and it is not likely to change for perhaps a generation. The pandemic has put business and social structures under enormous pressure, and research has shown how Covid-19 has revealed and accentuated the inequality gaps in the UK. It is easy to say that the virus has been non-discriminatory, but it has certainly impacted on some far more than others. Office of National Statistics research on the pandemic clearly highlights that the rates of infection and mortality were significantly higher among people from different ethnic backgrounds, and that they also fared the worst in employment outcomes.

Many, like Trevor Phillips, Founding Chair of the EHRC, have argued that business must change its approach in order to address skills gaps, recruit more widely and reflect the communities they serve.

'We know there is no shortage of qualified candidates to fill these roles if companies are willing to look,' he argues. 'Yet the snowy peaks of British business remain stubbornly white. This is not happening by accident. It is a consequence of what we do and what we do not do. That's why we cannot go back to business as usual.'

We also need to take into account an additional layer of complexity from a lens of intersectionality. The experiences of employees will not simply be based on differences in ethnicity, but challenges may be accentuated when set alongside gender, sexuality, socio-economic background, age or disability. It is becoming increasingly apparent that individuals are experiencing multiple forms of discrimination. This in itself is an indication of other social disadvantages and systemic inequality. A report by The Fawcett Society notes that women in particular are frequently unrepresented at board level.

'Women of colour are almost invisible from positions of power across both public and private sectors,' it concludes. 'They are overrepresented in entry-level and junior positions and virtually disappear the higher up we go into management and senior leadership. This does not happen in a vacuum – it is the result of structural racism and barriers faced at each stage in a woman of colour's career pipeline. The barriers experienced generate a cumulative impact and result in the erasure of women of colour at the highest levels.'

The report highlights that women from different ethnic backgrounds are twice as likely to be insecurely employed compared to white women, and take home a third less in pay than those on permanent contracts. It makes uncomfortable reading and concludes that people of colour, 'experience a number of barriers even before they are able to set foot into the labour market. Namely, intense discrimination at application and interview stage and racial biases in recruitment processes that lead to delays in entering employment, especially for graduates. They are also likely to be overqualified for the roles they occupy when they first enter the labour market, which is a particular problem for migrants of colour.'

However, while structural injustices remain, an increasing awareness of the benefits of what's been called a 'diversity dividend' is forcing business to confront prejudice and examine their culture. The benefits of smarter decision-making from diverse teams, as opposed to the complacency and sameness of thinking that homogenous collective thinking often produces, has long been championed by researchers.

Furthermore, with a 2020 Glassdoor survey showing that 76 per cent of job seekers said a diverse company was important when evaluating job offers, it is becoming clear that businesses will struggle to attract talent without an inclusive culture.

There are multiple reasons why diverse workplaces are desirable. These range from increased innovation, loyalty and retention, to reduced staff turnover, improved talent acquisition and an elevated company culture.

Arguably the most important reason, though, is that for businesses to succeed they need to understand their communities.

'I get quite irritated by the business case for diversity, not because I don't believe there is one, but I feel unbelievably strongly that the reason why we need to be more diverse and more inclusive is because it matters in its own right,' explains Dame Sharon White DBE, Chair of the John Lewis Partnership. 'Even if business was going to be as effective with a homogeneous culture, it is a matter of principle that we reflect the different perspectives of the entire country. When I was Chair of Ofcom, we were running really hard to catch up but we did that because it was the right thing to do, regardless of whether the business case stacked up.'

Despite the unforgiving experiences of some people across the business sector, there are others who do see an emerging culture of change, in part driven by a desire to attract the best talent. Dr Heather Melville, banker and Director of Client Experience at PricewaterhouseCoopers UK, has commented on changes she has seen in finance and professional services. She argues that some organisations are making great strides and should be commended for not shying away from discussions about race and racism. It is her view that some organisations genuinely care about creating an inclusive environment.

'There's an understanding that you can't just go to the same talent pools all the time,' she acknowledges. 'There are some organisations doing great things and they should be commended – and they're not shy to talk about the race word. Organisations that really care about creating an inclusive environment do it because they want the best talent and they want access to all the talent.'

Naturally, opinions are divided on whether a business being forced to adopt inclusive practices as a means to access talent and enhance their bottom line is a good enough indicator of change. There are many push factors driving business in this direction.

Whether it's the growth of social movements such as Black Lives Matter and Stop Asian Hate, global surveys showing people want business to take on a bigger societal role, or ESG (Environmental, Social, and Governance) criteria driving heightened expectations around diversity and inclusion or Government interventions such as the Parker Review, which seek to improve boardroom diversity, it is becoming more difficult for business to resist change.

But the question is whether business is merely paying lip service to this change, keeping the same calcified power structures in place along with an age-old toxic culture, while making token appointments in lower-paid roles. I have visited a number of companies where the walls are plastered with corporate pictures of Benetton-style images of workplace diversity that simply don't match up to the reality on the shop floor.

Those companies that really value diversity are building an authentic culture that's welcoming, respectful and eschews the well documented 'bro culture' that prioritises macho men and toxic behaviour, and is pervasive in many start-ups.

Of course, this is not easy and building a supportive and authentic culture takes time and hard work. And most importantly, it requires leadership commitment to drive it across every level of the company. It can't be something that's just left to HR to deliver.

Sadly, I spoke to many people who reflected a business culture that was unwilling to properly value and commit to inclusion.

People in different businesses representing a wide spectrum of industry spoke of frequently experiencing racism and micro-aggressions in the workplace.

Belonging, in particular, is a key human need that is all too often downplayed in the equality, diversity and inclusion (EDI) agenda. A feeling of acceptance and being valued has to be core to an agenda that promotes an inclusive environment. Micro-aggressions are not always intentional but can be very harmful. The common defence for micro-aggressions in the workplace is that it is 'just banter', but the unease that this can cause is as impactful as more overt forms of racism.

Micro-aggressions more generally, and everyday racism, are not widely discussed in the workplace. As a result, the reporting levels of racist incidents remains relatively low. In many cases, employees are not just experiencing single incidents of discrimination but a series of less overt occurrences. The accumulative impact on individuals is difficult to determine. But the impact on mental health and wellbeing is likely to be one of the first symptoms.

There is insufficient research focusing on the day-to-day experiences of people from different ethnic backgrounds in the business sector, but there is no shortage of anecdotal evidence. It is often difficult to prove cases where an individual has been subjected to excessive scrutiny by colleagues and managers. Barriers to promotion and development, or the absence of additional opportunities, can sometimes be justified by other means. The denial of opportunities has a significant impact on the promotion and progression pipeline.

Dianne Greyson, founder of the Ethnicity Pay Gap campaign, explains how micro-aggressions have come to be seen as 'acceptable racism'. 'I think a lot of the things that troubled me in the office were micro-aggressions. Stuff like touching my hair and saying things like, "Are you going to have rice and peas tonight?" These are more irritating than anything else.' She also notes that race tropes such as the 'angry black woman' were prevalent and that this was often used defensively when other employees failed to perform basic duties. 'If I asked someone to get some information for me, which was a legal requirement, I would be ignored. Then when I politely asked again, I was told I was aggressive.'

These constant stings and barbs are increasingly prevalent in the business sector. 'In the world we live in today, people don't tend to do overt racism,' explains Dr Heather Melville. 'It's very cleverly done and you feel it. There's a real sense of being different. So, it's things like [when people ask]: "Where do you really live? Where did you really go to school?" Or if you're wearing a nice piece of jewellery or have a nice bag, they ask, "Is that real?" So, it's all these micro-aggressions. "Did you really work at xy?"'

Warren Christian, who now works in business development, shared his experience of working in construction management. He said that at one stage in his career he was taunted and told to 'stop using big words' by one of the area directors. Although he enjoyed his career in construction overall, it was clear that his time was somewhat tainted by continued micro-aggressions. 'I'll never forget the face of the project manager when he realised our international construction company actually had a black manager such as me,' he recalls. 'I knew it would be the beginning of my problems and this seeded feelings of anxiety.'

The feeling of being different and not fully accepted are a common theme to those who are 'othered', and one that is some-times viewed as being uncomfortable to challenge. In some cases, people have adopted a strategy of simply not focusing on the inap-propriate behaviours or comments. In other cases, there has been an approach to resilience based on the hope that 'it will all sort itself out in the end'. Such coping strategies should not be seen as being evidence that those on the receiving end are comfortable with the situation. Rather, the opposite is true. A degree of sadness may indeed lie beneath. A respondent to my research commented that there is 'a feeling of sadness when you realise you'll never be fully accepted by those who want to maintain divisions'. He went on to add, 'I recall the general manager giggling to other senior staff members about one chap's attire and accent. He was a devout Muslim, who was an exceptional staff member; however, this was of little reference. This "them and us" mentality would be a constant theme throughout my career.'

The respondent reiterated that despite experiencing these inci-dences frequently, he had optimism in the movement towards a fairer more accepting culture, but voiced concerns about the pace of change. The need to increase the rate at which change happens was universally felt by all those who shared their experiences.

Other feedback from senior figures who wished to remain anonymous showed how many placed a heavy emphasis on building personal resilience as a coping mechanism to deal with the prevalence of micro aggressions. 'I volunteer as a mentor to youngsters getting into business, and resilience,' one explained. 'Building confidence in one's own ability and the acceptance of a greater good are the ways in which I have dealt with the challenges arising from this despicable behaviour.'

One business founder said her experience of micro-aggressions was that they extended into putting pressure on her to run diversity forums in the company. 'When I told them I didn't have time because of my workload, I was told I wasn't being supportive of my race,' she said.

Ranjana Bell MBE, who has over 35 years' experience working in the field of equality and diversity, explained that her approach to challenging discrimination has been directly influenced by the experiences of her parents. 'Watching my mum being treated so disgracefully by her bosses, in the shops, by the cruel looks and comments and being excluded . . . . I started challenging things at a very early age. My mum told me to "turn the other cheek". I wouldn't do it then and I will not do it now.'

There is a new generation coming through that have similarly witnessed their parents tolerate abuse and discrimination, and are not prepared to go through the same ordeal. As a result, abuse in the workplace that their parents turned the other cheek to is unlikely to go unchallenged anymore. Research from the Chartered Institute of Personnel and Development shows that people from different ethnic backgrounds are more likely to say that progression is an important part of their working life than their white counterparts. However, BAME employees are more likely than white

British employees to say their career progression to date has failed to meet their expectations.

Mitie Group CEO Baroness Ruby McGregor-Smith was appointed by Government to lead on the Race in the Workplace Review and has highlighted that people from different ethnic backgrounds, particularly those of African and African-Caribbean heritage, are too often stuck in junior management roles.

'Barriers exist, from entry through to board level, that prevent these individuals from reaching their full potential,' she explained. 'This is not only unjust for them, but the "lost" productivity and potential represents a huge missed opportunity for businesses, and impacts the economy as a whole. The potential benefit to the UK economy from full representation of people from different ethnic backgrounds across the labour market, through improved participation and progression, is estimated to be 1.3 per cent of GDP.'

Ravi Vekaria, Managing Partner of Assetree Group noted that it was only during his early career in banking that he started to see differences in the ways that people from different ethnic backgrounds were treated. 'Asians appeared to be in support roles and whites seemed to have had the graduate schemes,' he observed. 'All my managers, their bosses and bosses' bosses were Caucasian.'

Another person who contacted me to share their experiences in the workplace highlighted the power of positive role models in senior roles.

'I am a great believer that positive role models in the ethnic minority communities can and do have an enormous positive effect,' he said. 'We need more of this so those without any positive role models can understand and appreciate that others have travelled similar journeys and gone on to excel.'

This is something I relate to, and others have spoken about the pressures of trying to reach senior roles when there are no people of colour as role models to assure them it can be done.

Turkish-born Design Director Melin Edomwonyi spoke about feeling similar pressures in a BBC interview when setting up her own business after spending 15 years in the creative industries. She described feeling pressured to be a visible role model to other young entrepreneurs and admitted to wanting 'people of colour, young people . . . to feel encouraged and to see what I didn't see when I was growing up'. In the same interview, Cardiff University graduate Azaria Anaman remarked, 'I know of an entrepreneur who has a jewellery business, like diamonds and jewels and such, and on their social media page they wear gloves so they can't see the colour of their skin.' Highlighting the successes of people from diverse ethnic backgrounds will be an important way to give visibility and elevate those around us. Nobody should feel they have to play down or hide their ethnicity or the colour of their skin.

Beyond seeing people of different ethnic backgrounds in senior roles as a source of inspiration, this lack of visibility can have further consequences on the broader culture of a business. Research by Henley Business School found that 33 per cent of employees felt that a lack of diversity in leadership was driving racial inequity and systemic racism within businesses.

Diversity at C-Suite level presents an interesting picture. While there is some movement at entry level in terms of changing demographics, companies generally get paler as you look towards higher levels, or 'snowy peaks'. Those from ethnic minorities who do manage to break through to higher levels seem to face a more challenging path than their white counterparts. The pipeline of diverse talent appears to be slowly changing around the margins but there is little change to mainstream progression routes. As of 2022, ethnic minority representation in Chief Executive, Chief Financial and Chair roles stood at 3.7 per cent. This amounts to an increase of one additional ethnic minority leader since 2014.

At first glance the steadily changing demographic of representation of people from different ethnic backgrounds at Board level appears to suggest an improving picture. However, significant challenges still remain. As we know all too well, changes to the demographics around the table do not necessarily translate to meaningful inclusion or engagement.

The barriers to joining a board persist and the criteria for paid roles intensifies further. Unambitious targets such as one person of colour on every board by 2021 is unlikely to do much to change the enduring perception of an 'old boys' network'. If anything, it will only strengthen a view of tokenism, and this perception will reduce the likelihood of individuals putting themselves forward. For those who do put their name forward, opportunities to advance can often seem inaccessible due to criteria such as 'previous experience at board level' and the requirement for the candidate to be a suitable 'fit'. The gatekeeping stems the flow to board level and there are no guarantees that voices will be heard even if they manage to find a way past these obstacles.

So how then can we address too many examples of glacial progress and move faster on making lasting change?

A starting point for renewed impetus can be found in Henley Business School's report, 'The Equity Effect', which explored the impact of diversity and inclusion in UK businesses. The report sought to understand the reasons why racial inequity still exists in the workplace, and what the barriers and challenges are to overcoming it. Research included a survey of over 500 business leaders and 1,000 employees, asking questions about their experiences of race and racism in their workplaces and the measures their companies have in place.

It highlighted that businesses, actively confronting 'inequity and racism with practical measures, can expect to see an improvement in their employees' job satisfaction, loyalty, creativity and, ultimately, value, recording an average revenue 58 per cent higher across three years than those which did not.'

There has been a trend towards including unconscious bias training for new staff members across many companies. Some of these, including Starbucks, Google and Papa Johns, have been open about their commitment to the training, but it is not without controversy. In some cases, this is for all new staff as part of induction but in other cases it is confined to employees who are part of the recruitment and selection process. It should be noted that there are mixed perspectives on the impact of such interventions. The EHRC suggests that the ability of unconscious bias training to meaningfully change behaviour is limited and 'there is potential for back-firing effects when UBT participants are exposed to information that suggests stereotypes and biases are unchangeable'. While some companies remain committed to unconscious bias training, there has been a notable move in the opposite direction in the public sector. In December 2020, the UK Government published a 'Written Ministerial Statement on Unconscious Bias Training', which highlighted 'emerging evidence of unintended negative consequences' and also raised questions about the impact of broader diversity training. It reiterated a commitment to nurturing an inclusive environment but made clear that a preferred route was one that integrated the agenda through existing mainstream training provision. Concluding, it called upon other public sector agencies to review their approach and consider following suit. It remains to be seen if the approach gathers momentum in the business sector; however, the research certainly casts doubt over the design, consistency and efficacy of unconscious bias and diversity training.

Change in the sector is certainly not out of reach and the moral case for change should be the main driver for a paradigm shift that is sustainable. Lord Woolley, founder and Director of Operation Black Vote, has argued that opportunities and life chances can no longer be dependent on the colour of your skin or whether you're from the right background.

'We need all the talent we can muster to turbocharge UK plc,' he says. 'Using data to demonstrate inequalities really does work. Working with schools, universities, ministers, public servants and businesses, we have found an acceptance of most of the data, and a willingness to collaborate to put things right. It's difficult for powerful people and their institutions to say: "We got this wrong, we should change our approach, help us change it", without data.'

There also needs to be a whole community and whole organisation approach where everybody steps up to be part of the solution. Dianne Greyson emphasises the importance of supporting each other, with a focus on action. She feels that it's not enough to offer appreciation without considering further options for support and action. 'I find it quite offensive that there are other people like us who are in positions of power and do nothing to help others by lifting them up and elevating them,' she tells me. 'On the ethnicity pay gap, I see people who pop up and say, "Well done Diane", but they are not using the campaign or supporting it. I'm trying to help people and we need others to get behind it.' She strongly believes that behaviours, structures, policies and processes can all be barriers to change, and addressing one aspect in isolation will have limited sustainable impact. Diane does not underestimate the resistance to change and argues that reluctance is based on a fear that others 'will lose out if people of colour have a seat at the table'. She went on to reflect that some people think, 'they will lose their seat, lose money and people won't look at them the same way. It's not like that. We all win if it's fairer.'

Building these supportive networks where growing numbers help, support and advocate for fairer representation is key to driving change.

In an interview with ICAS' *CA* magazine, Sheree Atcheson, Global Director of Diversity, Equity and Inclusion at Peakon, commented that allyship 'should be about intervening, not just supporting; calling out inappropriate behaviour and taking a stand on micro and macroaggressions. We should be embedding allyship into businesses and creating appropriate policies that work for everyone.' This feeds into a broader sentiment that we should be demanding more from our employers, more from our allies and more from each other. All levels of an organisation need to be involved in order to avoid a disconnect between a vision for change and action.

In order to break the deadlock and move the needle to create lasting cultural change that goes beyond a tick-boxing exercise, it will be critical for businesses to review their model of resourcing. A whole organisation approach does not and should not come for free. One of our respondents noted that, 'Too many organisations want the "halo effect" of engagement rather than delivering real change. They want to look good rather than do good.' She added that until companies saw this as a central issues rather than a peripheral one, they would continue to tinker at the edges. 'I find hope in the fact that people have found a voice. But I want companies to stop adding workload onto minorities to fix the problem without a budget, yet they somehow find a budget for tables at the diversity awards ceremonies.'

The idea of a collective approach based upon mutual support has also been highlighted by Dr Heather Melville. She told me that the value of having senior men and women around her who have supported her based on her deliverables and outputs was indispensable. Her advice to young people would be to firstly recognise that they need more than just a great qualification, because to really get ahead, 'you need a trusted circle of people of different nationalities that can share some of your experience but also guide you in a way that you listen and hear what they're saying to you.'

This emphasis on the importance of having strong advocates came through repeatedly from feedback, and this is something that affects everyone. In one instance, we were contacted by a business leader, who highlighted that even people from diverse ethnic backgrounds can fall foul of making unfair judgements about others. In this case it was the respondent's partner who played a critical role in stressing the importance of mindful leadership with equality at the heart.

'A moment I wasn't proud of that I would like to share is that early in our journey, I judged someone's worthiness for a job because I couldn't pronounce their name on their CV,' he explained. 'My partner (now wife) – absolutely hammered me and cornered me to take responsibility and give the young man an interview, to which I did with pleasure. Her ferocious need to emanate equality is what set me on a path of mindful leadership and teamwork. I don't profess to ever be the saint in business, I still unconsciously make judgements, but I vow to always have my optics refocused or see things from other viewpoints regardless of gender, race and position.'

His honesty serves as a reminder that changing a long-established mindset of prejudice towards minorities is going to take much more than good intentions and a few diversity workshops.

Recognising the urgent need for wider research on the everyday experiences of racism in the business sector is arguably the first step towards efforts to shift a resistant culture and break outdated behaviours of the 'old boys' network'. What's more, we need more data on the reporting or barriers to recording incidents. Research by Henley Business School suggests that a fear of being judged is the primary reason for people not reporting racial discrimination. This suggests the data available is only giving us a partial picture and may indeed be the tip of the iceberg. A further aspect that is compounding the fear of being judged is the discomfort some white people feel about discussing racism in the workplace. Research suggests that in part this is due to a fear of using inappropriate terminology and causing offence. This has caused a perfect storm whereby low levels of open debate and low levels of reporting are blocking progress towards more inclusive corporate cultures.

The picture across the sector is inconsistent and there have certainly been signs of more progress in some areas over others. At the extreme end of the scale, the 'bro culture' that's become synonymous with tech companies is in many ways the antithesis to an inclusive business culture. Bro culture is often characterised as an environment where managers scream instructions, excessive partying and drug use is encouraged, and winning and success is placed above respect for others.

Stories of a chief operating officer dressed up as a black stereotype at company-wide 'gin and juice' parties, constant sexual harassment, and interview processes that make people feel like they are being asked how as a black person they can fit into this environment have sadly become all too commonplace.

Progress is being made, however, but it is slow and uneven. It is encouraging that 89 FTSE 100 companies are now more representative then they were five years ago, according to the Parker Review. However, there are still too many businesses that see themselves as leaders in diversity, simply based on an approach of recruiting more people from different ethnic backgrounds while doing little to change their culture. We still have a long way to go in some quarters before we develop a more widespread appreciation that this is not just a numbers game. More specifically, diversity in a workforce does not guarantee inclusion. We need greater scrutiny of the level at which new ethnic minority recruits join, the amount of time spent at each level before promotion, and more widespread reporting of the ethnicity pay gap. A key precursor to a paradigm shift is greater awareness of what is happening at the coalface. We need more voices speaking out on injustices on the shop floor, in the office and the boardroom. Above all, we need to acknowledge the range of experiences, learn, reflect and make sure UK plc is open to everyone.

7

PRIVILEGE

Some years ago, I was walking around one of Birmingham's poorest council estates with a friend. It was a sunny day in the south of the city and the cloudless sky was dominated by 15 tower blocks. Developed in the 1960s, Druids Heath had remained unchanged for over half a century and was the only large council estate in Birmingham that hadn't been subject to major development.

As we both looked up at the high rise buildings, which possess some of the worst levels of child poverty in the country, my friend turned to me.

'Do you know what I'm seeing in those flats?' he asked. 'Future CEOs, industry leaders, football managers, politicians, theatre directors.'

I smiled, knowing he was absolutely right to see the enormous potential of the children living there.

I also knew, having grown up a few miles away in a humble two-up two-down, that those towers would undoubtedly house big dreams – even if few people recognised them.

And that's the problem with talent these days. It's often only recognised when it speaks with the right accent, wears the right school tie or comes from the right part of the city.

Over recent decades I've seen the class divisions harden in Britain, social mobility go into reverse and a strange myopia sweep the nation. Where we once saw talent everywhere, we're now blind to it and actively ignore or discourage communities that are brimming with potential.

In so many different disciplines and sectors, I've seen working-class talent utterly squeezed out.

I saw cricket collapse as a working-class sport as so many state schools no longer play it and sold their playing fields off in the 1980s and 1990s. The game in this country is now dominated by privileged, privately educated players.

To a large degree, the same has happened in music. Once a bastion of upwards social mobility, where working-class talent thrived, it's now been taken over by a wave of privately educated acts. From Coldplay and Lily Allen to Florence Welch and Mumford & Sons, there's been a significant privileged cultural shift.

It's the same in the professions too. From accounting and engineering to law and medicine, societal privilege often trumps merit and makes sure you stay ahead. As the Government's own Social Mobility Commission acknowledged in 2021: 'Opportunities are still based on what your parents did. Today, you are still 60 per cent more likely to be in a professional job if you were from a privileged background rather than a working-class background.'

But even though it's blindingly obvious that so many of Britain's institutions and social structures are dripping with privilege and oozing with entitlement, our leaders are doing little to change this.

And it doesn't help that the very term privilege, or rather 'white privilege' has become highly politicised.

The notion of white privilege has longstanding origins. The American sociologist and civil rights activist, William Du Bois, wrote in the 1930s about the 'psychological wage' that enabled poor whites to feel superior to poor blacks. And then in the 1980s the anti-racism activist, Peggy McIntosh, wrote about it in an essay entitled 'White Privilege: Unpacking the Invisible Knapsack'. In this seminal work, she wrote about how she'd been taught about racism solely from the perspective of how it puts others at a disadvantage. She'd not been taught the other side to this, however, which is how white privilege puts her at an advantage.

White privilege, she explained, was 'an invisible package of unearned assets, which I can count on cashing in each day, but about which I was "meant" to remain oblivious. White privilege is like an invisible weightless knapsack of special provisions, maps, passports, code books, visas, clothes, tools, and blank checks'.

Her work also listed 46 examples of white privilege, including the following examples.

4. When I am told about our national heritage or about 'civilization', I am shown that people of my colour made it what it is.

21: I am never asked to speak for all the people of my racial group.

24: I can be pretty sure that if I ask to talk to the 'person in charge', I will be facing a person of my race.

More recently it's been adopted by the Black Lives Matter movement to ascribe positive attributes or advantages to a person simply because of the colour of their skin.

If this doesn't sit comfortably with you, then you only have to look at the makeup of the workplace and the structural bias against people of colour.

Go into any major corporation and look at the cleaners. The majority will be people of colour.

Five years ago, in 2017, an independent Government-backed review by Baroness McGregor-Smith examined the challenges faced by black and ethnic minority talent in the workplace.

It acknowledged that people still find it hard to talk about race and ethnicity and concluded that people of colour 'are more likely to perceive the workplace as hostile, they are less likely to apply for and be given promotions and they are more likely to be disciplined or judged harshly'. And in a clear nod towards the privilege that many enjoy, it noted: 'In many organisations, the processes in place, from the point of recruitment through to progression to the very top, remain favourable to a select group of individuals.'

But, while writers, activists and academics have been talking about white privilege for decades, there are many who not only oppose it but want any mention of it silenced. The most notable of these opponents was Boris Johnson's Government. Ministers have warned that schools cannot discuss this in the classroom and should not support Black Lives Matter.

Naturally, this has generated lots of headlines and it's been used to pit poorer white children against people of colour, as ministers have argued that white working-class pupils are being neglected as a result.

Of course, it's true that a white working-class child on a run-down council estate is unlikely to feel privileged – but the Government has done nothing to address this and their policies are making inequalities worse. And dragging white working-class people into a culture war is not going to help anyone – except, of course, those from a tiny Oxbridge caste that wish to protect their privilege.

Over the last few years I've seen ministers weaponise the white working class and imply that those campaigning to lift people of colour and tackle structural racism are conspiring against white people. This is a shameful low. But, sadly, it's become the new modus operandi for the political right. The pathetic playbook of so-called strongman rulers such as Trump, Orbán, Putin et al. is to foster resentment and grievances, and sow division everywhere – and it's one that's been slavishly followed by our Government.

The fact that a white working-class man in Salford is on a zero hours contract and is struggling to pay his mortgage is certainly not the fault of a young Asian woman five miles away in Longsight, who lost her job in the pandemic and cannot feed her children. Both should be allies in the fight against a rigged system that ensures opportunity is unevenly shared and protects privilege at all costs.

Yet, while the Government's own Social Mobility Commission acknowledges that nearly one in three children in the UK now live in poverty, and that the pandemic risks worsening social mobility, I've seen little urgency to address this.

Instead of spreading opportunity, our leaders continue to concentrate it in the hands of a privileged few. And instead of creating an even playing field where everyone has a chance to get on in life, structural injustice is getting worse. People find themselves held back and working harder than ever for less return.

The pandemic has exposed and amplified inequalities, shining a harsh light on the reality facing many people of colour in Britain. Ethnic minorities experienced greater amounts of death from Covid-19 compared to the white British population and were also twice as likely to be living in poverty. Reports by the Living Wage Foundation have also shown that BAME workers are more likely to be in low paid and insecure work – such as having too few hours, zero hours contracts, or short notice of shift patterns – than white workers. When you also consider that Government figures show ethnic minorities were also most likely to live in the most deprived 10 per cent of neighbourhoods in England – and that people from the white British, white Irish and white other ethnic groups were the least likely out of all ethnic groups to live in the most income-deprived 10 per cent of neighbourhoods, a clear picture of the divide emerges.

But here's the thing about privilege: it's complex. While it's clear that most people of colour don't benefit from it in Britain, a tiny amount of people of colour in public life are frequently used to argue the opposite. How can Britain be racist when the Chancellor of the Exchequer has brown skin, people argue?

The answer is that Rishi Sunak has benefitted from the one thing that always provides a head start and allows you to take a place at the front of the queue. That is, of course, extreme wealth.

Privately educated, Sunak went on to become an investment banker and hedge fund manager before entering Parliament. Married to a billionaire heiress, he is said to be the richest MP in Britain and, according to *The Times*, was a multimillionaire by the time he reached his mid-twenties.

In my conversations with other ethnic minority Tory parliamentary candidates, it's clear there's a feeling of resentment that Sunak didn't have to earn his political stripes and fight a difficult seat before being given the opportunity to contest something more winnable. Instead, despite having no connections to Richmond, Yorkshire, he was parachuted into the safest Tory seat in the country.

Sunak is not the only wealthy ethnic minority in Parliament that a young Asian in Luton or a black man in Wembley would struggle to relate to. Kwasi Kwarteng, the son of Ghanaian immigrants, who was schooled at Eton, Cambridge and Harvard, is another. When he tried to defend the Government's handling of the Windrush deportation scandal on Channel 4, he was angrily challenged by the grime artist, Marci Phonix, who was debating with him on the same programme.

'You are not coming from the same place I'm coming from,' Phonix shot back after Kwarteng said he didn't know of anyone who had been deported. 'You don't represent the same people I represent. You would not know. And you don't care . . . It's a job for you . . . This is reality for me. When I leave here, my car can get pulled over for no reason . . . When I go in a shop, or my daughter goes in a shop, who's 12, she gets followed around the shop.'

It's yet another reminder that in the race to the top, we don't always get the leaders we deserve.

The first black Conservative MP, Adam Afriyie, said to be sitting on a £100 million fortune, famously raised eyebrows in an interview with the *Evening Standard* when he said, 'I don't see myself as a black man' and that he considers himself 'post racial'. More astonishingly, he claimed, we are 'heading rapidly towards a colour blind society'.

If only that were the case.

These are the words of a man who has let extreme wealth cut himself adrift from a reality shared by millions of people of colour.

And, in many ways, they exemplify how a reality of plummeting social mobility is one that's becoming invisible and unrelatable to those that are insulated by privilege.

It shows how far we've fallen as a country. For as long as we're blind to privilege, and treat leadership solely as a greasy pole to be climbed to achieve power, instead of a platform to relate and connect with people to empower them, then we'll continue to be a country where potential is criminally wasted.

And yet it doesn't have to be this way. For, as the American activist and author bell hooks pointed out, privilege is not in and of itself bad. 'What matters is what we do with privilege,' she argued. 'I want to live in a world where all women have access to education, and all women can earn PhDs, if they so desire. Privilege does not have to be negative, but we have to share our resources and take direction about how to use our privilege in ways that empower those who lack it.'

Back in Birmingham, my walks in the south of the city will no longer be guided by tower blocks on the skyline. Druids Heath is finally getting some attention from the Council and a seven-year development plan is well underway. The Council intends to demolish six tower blocks and re-house residents with a new masterplan earmarked for the estate.

Hydraulic excavators have already begun to tear down the blocks and, as the demolition jaws began to bring down the iconic buildings, amazing drone footage exposed the hidden details of those that lived there. A little girl's painted pink bedroom suddenly emerged in a shower of plaster and brick and you could see floral wallpaper and a vibrant red wall.

When I heard about this, I began to wonder where she and everyone else in that block had gone to. What hopes had they taken with them of a better life? Will they dream as high as the buildings they once occupied? Or will they too be bulldozed to ruins?

As I watched floor by floor slowly collapse, I couldn't help but marvel at how easily big structures can be destroyed. Tearing down the walls of injustice, however, will be an altogether bigger ask.

8

RELIGION

For by him all things were created, in heaven and on earth, visible and invisible, whether thrones or dominions or rulers or authorities – all things were created through him and for him. And he is before all things, and in him all things hold together. (Colossians 1:16–17)

The shadows were falling at Lambeth Palace when I made my way through the gatehall into the double-height hypostyle room. I hesitated for a second, soaking up the opulent surroundings and scanning the artefacts in the vitrines of the mezzanine gallery. But there was no time to lose myself in 800 years of history as I was ushered on towards a magnificent room that wouldn't have looked out of place in a film about Henry VIII.

And there he stood, his hand outstretched and a warm smile creasing his face.

'Welcome Nazir,' said the Archbishop of Canterbury, Justin Welby. 'We have a lot to talk about.'

Indeed we did.

As far back as I can remember, religion has always been important to me, and my faith has helped me through many difficult times. As a child, I was always taught to respect all faiths, and the influence of the Church of England was something I understood from a young age.

Whether you're religious or not, it affects all of us because Christianity and the Church inform almost all aspects of our national life. Be it our constitution, language, architecture, law, music, art or even our calendar, everything is influenced by Christianity. Our monarch is the Supreme Governor of the Anglican Church and the State; most of our national holidays are related to religion; and Britain still has a sizeable number of faith-based schools. To understand Britain, you have to fully grasp its Christian heritage and the Church's central role in our national life since the Reformation.

The Anglican Church has been the nation's core since the sixteenth century, but it's fair to say its influence is weakening, as Church of England attendance has been in slow and steady decline for decades.

At the time of our meeting, evidence from the UK's Office for National Statistics showed that the number of Christians in England and Wales was close to falling below half of the population for the first time. The 2011 census figures were updated in December 2021 and revealed that both nations are heading towards becoming majority non-Christian by 2050. As powerful as the Church's influence is, it is not unreasonable to question the validity and relevance of a national institution that attracts less than 2 per cent of the national population to regular worship.

There are, of course, many reasons for this, not least the growth of secularism. But with only 1 per cent of people aged 18–24 identifying as Church of England according to a British Social Attitudes survey, it's clear that this decline is generational. Put simply, many associate the Church as being represented by an out-of-touch cadre of middle-aged white people, who simply don't connect with or represent modern Britain.

When I put this to the Archbishop, he was quick to acknowledge the scale of the problem but insisted the Church was welcoming and inclusive.

'I'm driven by my faith and I remember that God reaches out to all of us and that's always been my point of view,' he says. 'And that means that we are all equal under God. If we are not doing it then we are not living up to his purpose for humanity.'

But if the Church does not appear to be inclusive, I suggest, because it suffers from poor representation of ethnic minority and black leadership positions, then surely it will alienate many in Britain's richly diverse cultural and racial landscape?

He nods. 'We have made a conscious effort to recognise inherent biases,' he admits.

'I believe that generation Z and the younger congregants have no time for discrimination and they know that there is white privilege. They know that you are more likely to be stopped and searched if you are black, they know how poverty and discrimination is embedded in our society.'

A few years back, while George Floyd protests were taking place worldwide, John Sentamu stepped down from his post of Archbishop of York. It meant that, for the first time in more than a quarter of a century, there was no black or minority ethnic diocesan bishop serving in the Church of England. At a time when racial injustice was taking centre stage, it was a clear indicator of how far the Church had fallen behind.

The aftermath of George Floyd's death and the Black Lives Matter movement subsequently ignited a long overdue sense of urgency to the experiences of black and ethnic minorities in Western societies. In the Church, many of those in leadership positions finally examined their treatment of people of colour and minority ethnic groups. All institutions have had to re-examine racial injustice and white supremacy in their midst. The Church's clergy made bold public statements in support of those fighting for racial justice. But I'm keen to understand how much of that has translated into action and whether Welby thinks enough progress is being made.

Certainly, current figures in relation to UK minority ethnic senior leaders within the Church of England are finally rising. 'Of 115 bishops, 5 are people of colour, although I've just announced 2 more,' Welby explains.

Change across the Church, however, is starting from a very low base. Some 11.4 per cent of candidates for ordination are from a minority ethnic background, which represents an increase of 6.2 per cent from seven years ago. But only 4.1 per cent of paid clergy identify as people of colour. A further 94 per cent of senior staff are white British.

'In other senior positions, 3 out of 140 archdeacons, 1 out of 43 deans, and 3 out of 86 canons are now people of colour,' adds Welby, noting, 'That's clearly not good enough.'

He says the Church has tried a very bureaucratic system to improve diversity over the last 30 years and it has not worked. As a result, he's now having to take more radical action to broaden his Church.

'Deliberate action is necessary,' he argues. 'Lots of appointments will come to me to sign off and I will get bunches of letters simply requiring a signature, but I started sending them back and requiring more information about the long list and the shortlist and breakdown by ethnicity, gender and disability and so on. Some of them refuse to do it, mostly white males. So, I refused to sign. There has been a bit of a standoff where appointments were not being made because I was not approving them and there's a lot of grumbling despite the fact that I was letting one or two pass which were desperately urgent. I remember my Chief of Staff being told that I was "politically correct Welby" but it was necessary for me to turn up the heat.'

This has put him in direct opposition to powerful conservative voices and seen considerable criticism flow his way. 'The Church of England's Diversity Mission has Gone Too Far', argued one *Spectator* headline. 'The Church of England is Institutionally Woke', read another one from *The Telegraph*.

Welby takes a different view, though, and in 2020 said the Church of England was still 'deeply institutionally racist'. If he is ruffling feathers by trying to push reform further and faster then so be it.

'I've heard that white men have said it's not fair,' he says with a shrug. 'But I say the last 500 years have favoured white males since the Reformation and I'm just applying the same standard to people of colour.'

Under new rules, Welby will not ratify appointments unless one BME and one disabled person is on the shortlist. Again, this has seen him run into difficulties.

'I learned that there were racist comments being made on selection panels because panels appoint people who look like them,' he admits, adding that 'One of our supplement Bishops said to an Asian person, "You wouldn't fit in round here" when he was applying for a job. Fortunately, I heard about it and that Bishop never forgave me for saying that he was not a good bishop and I ordered retraining for him.'

These continuing examples of deeply rooted prejudice forced him to take further action and create the independent Racial Justice Commission chaired by Lord Boateng.

This will see a commission of independent advisers scrutinise the Church of England's policies, practices and culture in relation to racial justice, reporting back to Welby with recommendations to help him root out systemic racism.

You can hear the frustration and shame in his voice as he tells me this. Just as there was when he addressed the General Synod and apologised for racism in the Church, adding that unless decisive action was taken now, 'we will still be having this conversation in 20 years' time and still doing injustice.'

I sense a restlessness in him to make progress and get things done and he says that unless others feel his shame then real change won't happen.

'I noticed that the CMEAC [Committee for Minority Ethnic Anglican Concerns] report have made 136 recommendations and only 2 have been put into action,' He sighs. 'Nobody owned it, because there was not enough embarrassment. We hadn't tackled the grassroots pipeline.

'I'm hoping that the public commission recognises how important embarrassment is because people tend to act when they are facing consequences.'

And, as I would find in the course of many discussions with religious leaders across Britain, there is much to be embarrassed about.

Last year's BBC *Panorama* documentary, 'Is the Church Racist?', about widespread racism in the Church, is a good starting point. The documentary revealed that those who complained of racism were paid off in return for their silence over the matter by signing a non-disclosure agreement. One of the clergy interviewed told *Panorama* he was warned that he would not find a job anywhere else if he complained about racism.

There have been many other awful examples of ethnic minority religious figures being ostracised. In the summer of 2020, for example, Augustine Tanner-Ihm, an ordinand, tweeted a rejection letter he received from one parish, which told him 'the demographic of the parish is monochrome white working-class, where you might feel uncomfortable'.

When I spoke to Manchester and England's first black cathedral dean, Rogers Govender, he voiced similar sentiments and pointed out that any challenge around the pervasive culture of the Church of England was usually met with resistance.

Recounting his journey in the institution, he began by explaining how he applied for the Archdeacon role in 2005 and said it's important to note that this role is above a parish priest, a canon, but below the Dean, the supplicant Bishop, ordinary bishops and the Archbishop. There is a statutory framework that applies to promotion and progression.

The Dean brought with him a wealth of experience from South Africa where he oversaw an area of 500,000 people and was also a liberation theologist. When applying for this role, there was only one other candidate, a British white man, who was considerably less experienced. The Dean had also been a parish priest for 15 years in the UK and was surprised to learn that he was overlooked for the post.

Understandably, he asked the Bishop why he didn't get the job and was taken aback to receive a frosty response for having the temerity to question the decision. In the Dean's opinion, the only difference was the race of the candidates. He complained that people of colour were being used as 'window-dressing' but not given any leadership jobs. He threatened to take this further but was then told that there was another vacancy that might be available as the Dean of Manchester.

It was the Dean's view that the Bishop was fearful of inflicting him on a primarily white congregation, where the Dean of Manchester's role was not a location specific one. He attended the senior appointments panel at Lambeth Palace in London for an interview and was appointed a couple of months later.

Looking back now, it was obvious to him that had he not made a fuss, he would not have been chosen. He put the fact he did down to his liberation background, which meant he had less deference towards senior leaders.

According to Govender, if the system is challenged or questioned by anyone then they are ignored. That usually means not being shortlisted for a few jobs until it becomes clear that there is nothing available for that applicant. He believes that the Church looks for a 'safe pair of hands' and highlighted how the Anglican Minority Ethnic Network (AMEN), an institution created for Church personnel, which offers mentoring, and support, is viewed by senior leaders as a 'bunch of troublemakers'.

Govender is of the firm view that, 'they are always your friends until you become their competition', and says an entrenched and outdated culture needs to be dragged kicking and screaming into the twenty-first century.

'They need to do different things in order to change the status quo,' he argues. 'If you look you will find and it is necessary to break the habits that are currently being pursued.'

Echoing the Archbishop of Canterbury's expressed desire to 'turn up the volume' to increase opportunities for ethnic minority clergy, he believes that intentionality is the key and instead of setting quotas, targets should be set which then have to be met.

Ultimately, though, large parts of the Church's thinking is pickled in aspic. Many believe there is a set image of a bishop as a white middle-aged man and as long as this perception endures then resistance to change will continue.

I spoke to others about this point, including the Bishop of Manchester. He conceded that he had been reflecting on racism in the Church and recognised that he had been given opportunities by others because he looked a little bit like them. 'Particularly in my earlier career,' he explained, 'powerful white men would have seen in me a potential protégé to encourage and provide with opportunities. It was only when, perhaps about 20 years ago when I began to hear repeated stories from people with very different backgrounds from my own regarding the struggles that they had faced in their own careers, that I began to reflect on my own advantage.'

Recognising that he is 'now in a position of considerable influence, both in directly appointing people to "pipeline" positions and in being able to give people career enhancing opportunities outside of their formal responsibilities,' he said, he was committed to changing appointment processes to undo years of bias.

'That begins by making robust efforts to ensure a very diverse range of candidates are identified for a particular vacancy and then ensuring that interviewing panels, exercises required of candidates etc. are all carried out in ways that encourage diversity,' he explains. 'I've found in practice that doing that well does result in very diverse appointments, notwithstanding that the final decision must be for the person who is the best fit for the role.'

The Church is clearly on a steep path of change and the Bishop readily admits that most of this is basic stuff that everyone should be doing, but 'it never ceases to amaze me how many instances I come across when people don't seem to make efforts to reach beyond their own "lookalikes".

I was frequently struck by the honesty of these conversations. But while people were largely making the right noises, I know that good intentions alone are never enough. In every discussion I had where religious leaders acknowledged that prejudice still persists, I could hear the Archbishop of Canterbury's words in the back of my mind playing like a continuous loop.

Unless action is taken now, we will still be having this conversation in 20 years' time and still doing injustice.

To date, 20 reports have examined the issue of racism within the Church of England over the last 35 years or so, making countless recommendations. Given the effort made, you do wonder why there remain significant barriers preventing black and ethnic minority groups from progressing in the Church. The Church has been proactive about making a change for many years but the progress is far too slow and too little. Embracing diversity is becoming increasingly important for the Church to revive some semblance of relevance in society as a whole.

It has, of course, been here before, though. The Church has had to examine its track record many a times in the past. Over a decade ago, the General Synod, Anglican Parliament, voted to issue an apology for the Church's involvement in sustaining the transatlantic slave trade. According to analysis of data collected by University College London, almost 100 clergymen benefitted from the trade. Of course the Church was not alone in these racist practices, as many of the other national institutions too were guilty of it over centuries, which means the history of all these institutions is inextricably linked with these injustices.

Why then does the Church remain rooted in a mindset of white supremacy – where subconsciously it considers whiteness to be superior – which then translates into most parishes across the country reflecting whiteness in Church leadership? The complicated association of Christianity with Englishness from our colonial past still reverberates in our present day.

Part of the problem here is that when talking about Christianity, race and diversity, many fall into the trap of thinking that Christianity is British or that it is European. In fact, Christianity isn't actually a white man's religion. It goes back centuries; one of the earliest churches is the Ethiopian Church, for example. And in the Bible itself, England didn't feature. We need to recapture and re-educate ourselves about what theology is and what Christianity is. It may seem like a radical concept but with Britain's changing landscape and increasing diversity, this will be a given (if it already isn't) in the not-too-distant future. It is something that can be worked towards gradually but consistently.

There also needs to be a wider understanding of how migrants have enriched faith and kept the Christian flame alight in this country. Many churches are dependent on migrant communities and hundreds of new Pentecostal churches have been started by black and other immigrant members. Research has shown that migrants are more than three times more likely than natives to attend a religious service weekly or to pray daily, while further UK Church statistics have shown that mass migration of Christians from countries such as Poland and Romania has helped stem the decline in church attendance.

This makes the disconnect between the Church and other races in terms of representation at leadership level all the more puzzling.

It's important to recognise that Church leadership does not just concern bishops. There are lay and ordained ministers in places such as parachurch organisations, mission agencies, theological colleges and diocesan administrators among many others. Unfortunately, even at that level, members are overwhelmingly white. This lack of diversity is not exclusive to the evangelical side, though. Leading Catholic organisations are no different.

But while the Church of England was frank in admitting its failings around diversity, I received no such acknowledgement from the Catholic Church.

Cardinal Vincent Nichols, the Archbishop of Westminster and President of the Catholic Bishops' Conference of England and Wales, told me that the Catholic Church was constantly mindful of the call of Pope Francis to ensure all are welcomed with dignity in our communities.

'The Catholic Church in England and Wales is committed to ensuring a real and helpful welcome to all who come to these lands, to protecting and promoting the unique contribution all are able to make with their distinctive culture so that all can fully integrate their lives here, in this place, and know that they have a home in the Church – in their Church.'

The fact that the Catholic Church is similarly experiencing a marked decline in attendance suggests, however, that many people still do not see it as 'their church'.

And Reverend Fr Paschal Uche, the first black British-born black priest of Brentwood diocese suggests the Catholic Church is losing people of colour because of this.

'I believe the Catholic Church leaks young black people either to other churches or to no church at all precisely because young black people may not have found a home in the Catholic Church,' he says. 'And it saddens me to say that but I believe it's the real experience for a lot of young black Catholics. You look at the clergy or the leadership, and the black population isn't represented there.'

After spending a good deal of time talking to business owners and public sector leaders driving through changes on diversity, I found it all the more baffling to see the Church struggling with the concept of equal opportunities and fairness. After all, this was an institution founded on the very fact that we are all equal before God.

Still it was clear to me that secular organisations have fared better when dealing with issues of race and diversity. The Church's complacency may emanate from it considering itself to have a heightened sense of morality – and assuming it would always do the right thing. It's also exempt from equalities legislation. The NHS and other national organisations have made strident progress in race and diversity, making the Church's attempts appear meagre in comparison. It would, therefore, do well to not only follow the secular organisations' lead but commit to a complete overhaul of vocation, training and appointments.

As the efforts of Welby and others noted here show, this is not to say that the Church has not been trying to accept where it has gone wrong, and it has shown the willingness to make the necessary changes. The reason why not enough has changed and the progress started is far too slow is because the willingness occurs more in principle than in practice. Millions have been spent on a 'renewal and reform' programme between 2017 and 2020, but a promise to 'reimagine the Church's ministry' has not yet seen transformative change.

The danger it poses is of a future in Britain where bigger barriers of misunderstanding could emerge between those with no religious affiliation and others with faith.

The letter to the editor by Stephen Cottrell, Archbishop of York, published in *The Times* in 2017, when his priesthood was as Bishop of Chelmsford, encapsulates the argument for Christianity's relevance and longevity.

'So much that we cherish in our public, political and cultural life flows from the Christian faith,' he argued. 'For instance, the belief that all people are created equal comes directly from the radically inclusive teaching of Jesus Christ. And . . . while these surveys tell us how faith communities and religious allegiances are changing, they do not change the Christian faith itself, or its power to enable people and communities to see themselves from a different perspective.'

The fact that, during the height of the pandemic, five million people tuned into an online service led by the Archbishop of Canterbury from his kitchen table should be a source of hope for the Church.

And while Britain may be becoming less Christian, it is by no means becoming less religious. Islam is one of the fastest-growing faiths and there has also been a significant increase, although less so than in Islam, in Hinduism and Judaism.

The human search for meaning, identity and principles that unite us as a society, however, have not gone away.

As a nation, I believe we still have a spiritual hunger but this must be matched by a similar appetite for change in our religious institutions. The Church, above all, needs to understand 'the fierce urgency of now' that Martin Luther King spoke of.

There are many recommendations in their reports that need acting upon – most notably the need for more participation in all places in the Church for people of different ethnic backgrounds. People of colour should be co-opted into the general Synod, which is the most senior governance body in the Church. Another recommendation is to get participant observers from ethnic minority backgrounds into the House of Bishops, which will help markedly in changing the environment and the actions of that group. Training, education and appointments is also highlighted. Seeing people of colour within the Church flourish will have ripple effects for the Church and wider society as a whole.

For years there has been a failure to provide appropriate service to many people because of their colour and ethnic background and this is very evident in the Church of England's positions of senior leadership. These are much less representative in proportion to black and ethnic minority MPs in Westminster and smaller in proportion to the ethnic minority Chairs and CEOs of FTSE 100 companies.

But while there has been too much handwringing and heels being dug in to resist change, there are some encouraging signs that change is beginning to look a more realistic prospect.

According to a recent statement from Church House, at least 10 clergy who are people of colour will be present at meetings of the House of Bishops within months. This was decided as a result of the Church's Standing Committee agreeing to a plan to address its lack of ethnic diversity. 'This may seem like a small step to some,' noted the Archbishop of York, 'but it ensures that a diversity of voices and experiences enriches the discussions of the House of Bishops as we seek to be a Church that truly embraces people of global majority heritage at every level of its life.'

There is certainly a long and hard road ahead for the Church, but, if continued, measures like this could well help counter the growing belief that the Church has failed to win the hearts and minds of people from different ethnic and racial backgrounds as well as the young.

And soon enough, small steps could eventually become leaps.

9

CIVIL SOCIETY

Creating richer social capital

I feel somewhat honoured to have spent my career both in public service and in civil society, but they're both sectors struggling with questions about identity.

While I have worked with some of the most committed and driven leaders, the lack of diversity is deeply concerning. If we accept the simple premise that leaders in the civil service and in the third sector can only truly represent the people they serve if they are representative of their community, then Britain continues to fall a long way short.

Prior to the pandemic, the institutional makeup of civil society was largely white and middle class, and while more charities are now engaged in EDI efforts, there is still a big gap between good intentions and practice. However, there's arguably a bigger need now to hold the third sector accountable for the lack of diversity in senior leadership positions. Not least because research from the National Council for Voluntary Organisations has shown that a good number of providers experienced a more diverse range of service users and an increase in the diversity of their volunteers during the pandemic.

This has yet to properly translate into meaningful change across the workforce or in leadership positions – and there are many reasons why. But, as I have found out, the fundamental problem remains the same in that more needs to be done to break the 'jobs for the boys' culture which still blights much of our civil society.

There is no doubt that there are individuals pushing to make a difference, but the change that is needed is held back by the prevailing culture.

Danny Sriskandarajah, CEO of Oxfam, says one of the reasons for this culture is that charities' socially important missions can blind them to serious failings.

'It remains shocking to me that the charity sector has a proportion of senior leaders that's even worse than that of business,' he says. 'It always troubles me that the charitable sector hides behind its mantra that "we are good people doing good" and therefore don't feel able to talk about things such as diversity, and particularly racism. We cannot just simply accept that people in the sector are good people doing good things; is there real accountability in the third sector when it comes to diversity? Trustees are often appointed by other allies because they look like them or went to the same schools or work in the same business, therefore the lack of diversity in the sector becomes self-perpetuating.'

He paints a scenario I've seen play out many times and which often creates a need for leaders to keep people dependent upon them. The developmental sector is often seen as the worst of the bunch and this culture results in white senior leadership working in countries that are predominately non-white. Critics have called it 'white saviour syndrome' and it's a label that sticks.

It's also a label that has begun to generate painful self-awareness of the problem within the sector. But, as Sriskandarajah explains, this doesn't always go much further than awkward hand-wringing.

'I walked into a room with 40 leaders at the launch of a "Charities So White" campaign where we were going to tackle the issue head on,' he says, 'and saw two of us were people of colour, which I thought wasn't bad, but I realised that the other one was simply the person doing the tech at the meeting.' He doesn't think much has changed, although, to his enormous credit, he tried.

One of the first things he did at Oxfam was to train about 40 members of staff as diversity champions. 'We ensured that no recruitment could take place without at least one of them being part of the process. We wanted them to ask questions about behaviours and to put out challenge.'

Then there were attempts to build a coalition of leaders to change things. 'I'm part of a WhatsApp group of CEOs of colour from the charity sector. It enables us to vent thoughts and to network. Maybe it's making me optimistic or maybe I'm just naive. We need to network more we need to support each other more. Something our white colleagues have done for years.'

Norms are shifting as a result. 'When we had a meeting of our CEO network of colour, I was torn between whether or not to post a picture of that network because I did not know how it would be perceived. Too often when we meet, or people of colour meet, there is a perception that we are up to something. However, we need to be out and proud. We need to ensure that people know we exist and that we engage.'

Establishing these sorts of structures and networks are really positive but, as it stands, there isn't the will and the drive among the current leadership to make it more widespread. Something is holding it back. His last remark about being perceived as 'up to something' when people of colour meet up is very common. I've experienced it myself many times. The worst outcome being when I found myself being investigated by the Metropolitan Police.

During my time as Director of Prosecutions for London, Chief Superintendent Ali Dizaei was a senior officer who the Metropolitan

Police suspected of corruption. He was later convicted of trying to pervert the course of justice, by my team. However, an earlier cack-handed attempt to get evidence of it led to him winning substantial damages from his bosses. They had to step away and let him progress to become Borough Commander in Hounslow, west London.

As fate would have it, somebody started impersonating him and extorting money from vulnerable small business victims from minority backgrounds. One of those intended victims approached me at a community engagement event and told me he had been approached by 'Dizaei' and asked to pay up unless he wanted to be arrested. The internet was not sufficiently established for him to have seen an image of the real 'Dizaei' at the time, but of course I had. Once I had satisfied myself that this was an imposter, I contacted Dizaei to tell him, as he was Borough Commander of the area where the imposter was operating. He immediately passed me to his Chief of Staff, which was entirely the appropriate thing to do, and he put an investigator on the case whom I introduced to the intended victim. Shortly afterwards, they set up a sting and arrested the fake. He was tried and convicted and sent to prison for several years.

Now what I didn't know for a while was that the Met Police had begun to investigate me. Why? Because I spoke to the real Dizaei about it. The fact that it led to an organised criminal being convicted was irrelevant. As one senior officer told me, 'Nazir spoke to Dizaei, they must have been up to something.' I was very angry, so much so that I wanted an apology from the Police and got a written one from Assistant Commissioner Yates. Whilst this is just an example, it is my firmly held belief that this sort of thing is commonplace. How many other times was a conversation between myself and another leader of colour perceived as plotting or maneuvering?

The fact that people of colour speaking to each other or networking is often perceived, consciously or subconsciously, in conspiratorial terms remains a serious barrier to progress.

According to research carried out by the campaign group Charities So White, only 9 per cent of staff in the charity sector are from black and ethnic minority backgrounds, and a further 92 per cent of Trustees and 97 per cent of CEOs are white. One of their contributors, 'Anika', illustrates the typical ethnic minority experience very well. 'They question my integrity, accuse me of having a personal agenda and say I use inflammatory language when I describe the problems of racism,' she observes, yet in the next breath, 'They tell me to educate white leaders and to find solutions to the problem.' She adds that, 'they fail to consider the emotional labour that they want to exploit and that it is, in fact, not MY job. Why should people of colour carry the burden of fixing the problem that white people have created?'

The NGO sector and smaller grassroots organisations have long played a critical role in plugging the gaps in provision that statutory agencies don't provide. Often founded on kitchen tables by extraordinary people who keep the most vulnerable safe, they are driven by a passionate thirst for justice and to solve deep-rooted social problems.

Yasmin Khan is one such example of an inspirational leader. I've witnessed the impact of the work she does heading up a northeast England based group that supports victims of abuse, mainly from minority backgrounds. Her experiences of how the sector manages diversity suggests there is still too much lip service paid rather than genuine attempts to embrace change.

'In my experience there is a complete lack of awareness from white senior leaders, who don't know how to treat BME leaders so they either become overly friendly or ignore me and my ideas all together,' she says. 'I find the institutional discrimination much more prevalent now, especially within strategic governance where I direct large organisations. Tokenism is a word I use carefully but it exists, which is why I am all for positive action but against positive discrimination.

'There is a real lack of understanding from boards and senior leaders, an unwillingness to change the way they work and address the real lack of meaningful engagement with BME groups. A statement at the end of the advert simply does not cut the mustard; knowing your communities is equally important as engaging with them. If I get asked one more time from a public body where they can recruit a more diverse board/staff I will run a mile!'

Again, it is uncomfortable for me to hear this, but it gets to the heart of the issue. Too often we see tokenism and organisations feigning support rather than putting the transparent and accountable structures in place to ensure they are nurturing and valuing diversity. That line at the end of a recruiting advert we're all familiar with – 'this organisation values diversity and encourages applicants from all backgrounds…' – is perceived as a get out of jail card to give the impression that the hiring process will be fairer, when it's often the opposite.

The charge of 'tokenism' was confirmed by many I spoke to, most of whom were afraid to go on record. The sense I got was that while diversity was something everyone agreed was a noble aim, there was little attempt to shape the culture to support it. And, as Danny Sriskandarajah explains, even when attempts were made to build such a culture, it frequently did not command wider support.

'Oxfam has a variety of clubs and societies but until recently we never had a network of minority staff,' he explains, 'so when one was set up I was keen to support it. They invited me to a committee meeting but found that all the rooms were booked and so I said let's all meet in the cafeteria. There we were sat in the cafeteria talking to each other and it was obvious that some people walking in were questioning what was going on. When I joined the queue to get some food and a colleague of mine introduced me to another member of staff, I was asked "Do you work in IT?" That took me back to the days when I attended the Commonwealth Club and always wore a suit and tie because I knew I did not want to be confused with the waiting staff.'

Perhaps the largest study of diversity in the charitable sector was the report delivered by the Association of Chief Executives of Voluntary Organisations (ACEVO) and Voice4Change in June 2020 titled 'Home Truths: Undoing Racism and Delivering Real Diversity in the Charity Sector', which took evidence, anonymously, from over 500 people across the sector. Its conclusion – that 'the charity sector has a problem with racial and ethnic diversity. BAME people are under-represented . . . and those who are in charities can be subject to racism and antagonism not faced by white colleagues' – was not surprising but grounded in the experiences of dozens of senior leaders. Its first recommendation that charities 'redefine racism as ordinary, systemic and institutional' didn't get anything like the attention it deserved. As the report found 68 per cent of BAME staff working in charities have experienced, witnessed or heard stories of racism in the sector, that's not a minority issue.

ACEVO commendably published a letter signed by 119 CEOs of charities committing themselves to eight leadership principles to address the issues identified in the report. These principles include, 'acknowledging that they have a problem', 'recognising that they need to model positive behaviours', and, interestingly, 'recruiting for potential, not perfection'. It's fine as far as it goes, but Sriskandarajah's experience, reflected by many others, is that they are seen as imposters as soon as they achieve roles of influence or power. 'We have been drafted in to make the organisation look good, no more, no less. It also means that the real power is somewhere else,' he argues.

This begs the question: where might that be?

Civil society is supported by the civil service and the diplomatic service, which is made up of hundreds of thousands of people managing the delivery of services on behalf of the public. Most start, like I did, in junior positions before climbing the ladder to reach more senior roles – the highest being permanent secretaries of Government departments.

I'm sure you know what I'm going to say before I say it here, but at the time of writing there are no people of colour in any of these 20+ top roles. There have, I believe, only ever been three in the history of the civil service. While the proportion of senior civil servants with an ethnic minority background has increased, the top-level permanent secretaries are all still white.

The diplomatic service is understandably more diverse given that we have to engage with people in foreign countries and need to speak their languages and recognise how their politics and cultures are evolving. Ambassadors and consular staff are the front line of all things British. Historically, that's meant white British, but as this country changed, so did the profile of these roles. Nobody that I reached out to was prepared to speak on the record, though some sought permission but were refused. So, I had to find a different route – and ask people I know.

Not surprisingly, they painted a familiar picture of applicants from certain schools and universities being prioritised for promotion, with a handful of people of colour progressing to some of the less important roles internationally. Junior staff compete in what they consider to be far from a level playing field where it's hard to progress.

'They are happy for us to network in official groups where a white senior official is the diversity champion, but the moment we set off on our own is the catalyst for questioning a lot our motives,' one told me.

Another senior diplomat was more blunt. 'They trust us when we're in low risk jobs in low risk territories, but they'll watch us like hawks if we're lucky enough to get higher positions in high-risk countries. It's as if they think we'll go native.'

We've heard before about strange conspiratorial assumptions when people from minority communities speak to each other in informal settings, but the assumption that we will suddenly become less British if we go to countries that are full of black or brown people is a troubling new threat.

It reflects a view that if we're British Asian, for example, we're less British than a white British person. I used to confront that view head on with the line, 'If you have two children it doesn't mean that you instinctively love one more than the other.' We can have multiple identities that don't conflict. However, there is clearly a school of thought that the "British" bit of "British Asian" must always triumph. The last time I checked, everybody who had spied for a foreign Government was white British. But we're seen as the threat!

This feeds into a worryingly narrow view of leadership that exists across large parts of the civil service, which is that leaders always come from a very select pool of talent. And until that talent pool is widened and leaders of a different mindset, background and/or ethnicity are recruited, then nothing will change.

'Change, respect and inclusion comes from the top,' explains Kausar Bibi, a senior civil servant who spent years working for the Home Office and was frequently posted abroad.

'I have spent years in a serious career with irreplaceable experience and qualifications, but the top jobs are always given to people who are white or went to Oxford or Cambridge and studied fine art or some other irrelevant field,' she added.

And without strong inclusive leadership, organisations are always susceptible to developing toxic cultures.

Relating some of her experiences in the civil service, she recalls one incident in her first week where a colleague shouted, 'What is she doing here? She does not belong here' across the desk.

'This verbal attack was extremely humiliating and unexpected. Not a single colleague came to my defence or asked me if I was OK having witnessed the event. It was ignored and was insulting to my dignity. I had joined with a positive and motivated mindset, only to be discriminated against for no reason. Since then, I have been constantly undermined by young graduates who are being groomed to be the next top civil servants but are culturally and professionally inadequate.'

Appointments to the civil and diplomatic services are through the Public Appointments Process, as are appointments to hundreds of boards which direct the provision of public services. This is a process that I have 'experienced' a number of times.

I use quote marks because the experience is like nothing I imagined. It's often just a process devised to give the appearance of fairness and equity without even a nod to the reality. On occasions it's blatantly used to appoint a preferred candidate, invariably white, but actively seeks people of colour to engage so it can turn round and say it was appointment in merit with a diverse field.

The department appointing is heavily involved in promoting it, shortlisting and interviewing. An independent commissioner chairs, but the question 'Is this the person you're looking for?' is commonly asked of the departmental director before deciding who is appointable. Then there is the master stroke. The final decision on appointment is made by the Minister, so even if you think you have a chance, it can be removed at the stroke of a pen. Look again at the dearth of persons of colour at permanent secretary and director level. Then remember that they are involved in deciding who their replacements will be. It's a self-perpetuating system that denies people from minorities from reaching the higher ranks.

My first experience of racism in a promotion board was 25 years ago and I didn't even know racism was in play because I naively believed that they were appointing the best person for the role. How do I now know there was racism? Because another person of colour who was also part of the selection exercise was braver than me and decided to pursue an employment tribunal when she failed to be appointed. Part of the evidence examined by the tribunal was the notes made by the interview panel. There in black and white, one white panel member had written 'troublemaker' at the top of the page before the interview had even begun. Other notes complained about the way she spoke. However, none of the white candidates had any pre-interview notes made. The tribunal found that racism had been a major factor in the decision-making. I tried to understand why I hadn't complained. Simply put, I was scared to death about the effect on my career.

The positive outcome was that the Director of Public Prosecutions, Sir David Calvert-Smith QC, immediately ordered an independent external inquiry which concluded that the organisation was 'institutionally racist'. Again, to his great credit, when the next big promotion opportunity arose, I was appointed as the first Muslim Chief Prosecutor and, even more extraordinarily, this was three months after the atrocity that was 9/11. At a time when being a Muslim led to suspicious looks, they appointed a Muslim. It was a serious statement of intent.

So far we have looked at the third sector and the civil service but toxic attitudes and cultures pervade all of our civil society. What about those who represent us, who advocate for us? I spoke to three union members who you will know from the more significant roles that they now occupy.

Naz Shah is the Labour MP for Bradford West, an area with a large British Pakistani population. 'Fifty per cent of my constituents are of British Pakistani origin and every time I raise an issue that relates to them specifically, I'm seen as playing the race card. Surely all I'm doing is representing my constituents.' That a serving MP feels this way is troubling in itself.

Naz talks about the need to work so much harder to get her voice heard and how being an ethnic minority MP can be exhausting. 'I was invited, along with a number of other MPs, to a small dinner with a visiting guest. I noticed that I had been relegated to a table right by the toilet whilst the other MPs were sat at the top table or near it. It felt like a teacher had told me to know my place.

I kept the seating plan as a memento of how it made me feel, to remind me that my very existence is challenging to some people. I wanted to leave the table and walk out, I wanted to cry, I had never felt so belittled, but I never raised it.'

This experience has helped to drive Naz on and she is clear about what needs to be done.

'Institutions regularly talk about being brave in their conversations,' she says, 'but it makes little difference to the diversity of their employees. I'm really concerned about target setting because it's often used as an excuse to achieve very little. There needs to be more roles for people of colour. It's not about special treatment, but it is about recognising the obstacles we face and supporting us in that process. But, ultimately, it's about changing culture and changing the psychology of leadership.'

Vaughan Gething was the Minister for Health in Wales during the pandemic and has been the Minister for the Economy since 2021. He has talked about the reality of racism, from growing up in rural west Devon to being one of the most prominent politicians in Wales during the pandemic. He believes that there is a 'significant level of responsibility on us to change things' and supports positive action. 'Visibility encourages more people into politics and you can only be what you see. We need to talk about disparities such as stop and search, but when we do too many white people become defensive.' Rightly, he believes that white people need to engage. 'I am glad that I've never been asked to be a Minister for Equalities and I wouldn't want that.'

Vaughan uses the example of trade unions and believes that employers need to ask themselves why their pipelines are so white. One woman seeking to change this is Shavanah Taj who has been General Secretary of the Wales TUC since February 2020. Shavanah has progressed to the top, but there have been plenty of obstacles before her. And, as she explains, the trade union culture is hardly a model of inclusivity.

'On my first day working for a trade union, a white middle-aged, male colleague approached me in an open plan office and asked loudly, "How do you feel about being recruited through the positive action programme?"' she recalls. 'There wasn't even a positive action programme, so now they're inventing programmes from which we are supposedly benefitting.'

Even though she has reached the position she has, she is clear that her pay and terms and conditions do not match that of other white colleagues doing the same job as her in other parts of the country.

A quick look at the leadership of trade unions is troubling. The TUC General Council is overwhelmingly white; union senior leadership is overwhelmingly white; union executive councils are overwhelmingly white; and their membership is proportionately people of colour. Why is this the case in 2022? We had leaders of colour going back to Bill Morris at the Transport & General Workers Union more than 30 years ago. There is no shortage of EDI strategies, no shortage of EDI staff and lots of talk. But where's the action?

I asked Shavanah, what would she do to reduce the impact of racism on the next generation of BAME leaders? 'We must create our own cadre, of BAME excellence that is intersectional, rich, diverse and accepting of all,' she says. 'We should actively mentor, support and offer opportunities to those coming up. We shouldn't accept every opportunity for ourselves but be willing to share space and pass across opportunities to those who are early in their journey of leadership.'

The Mayor of Liverpool, Joanne Anderson, was one of very few black or mixed race people in the area that she grew up in. Through her extensive experience in both the CPS and local Government, she has a clear view on what needs to be done to support ethnic minority leaders.

'You need to look at the whole process of recruitment, you need to ensure that networks exist to support future leaders and you've got to give them opportunities even when they may not necessarily have the experience of others,' she says. 'They cannot be allowed to fail, which is why you must support them and encourage them, train them and educate them. They cannot be special cases, however, otherwise that undermines the whole effort to improve the decision-making of the organisation.'

Whilst I recognise that there are genuine attempts to move things forward, the lack of diversity in our civil society is still alarmingly prevalent. Those BAME leaders that are driving the change have had to battle cultural and institutional prejudice throughout their careers. It can be exhausting. And things just-aren't changing quickly enough. This is a problem for all of us, whatever your background.

As Britain has struggled to escape a pandemic that has seen a sharp increase in deprivation and widened inequalities, the role of civil society has rightly become more appreciated. The head of the Government's levelling-up taskforce, Andy Haldane, has argued that this sector is key to strengthening social capital and needs to be valued more.

Recalling the words of William Beveridge in a report from 1948, who made the case for an enhanced programme of co-operation between the public sector and civil society, he says we have missed the opportunity to unlock this potential.

He is right that the 'fruitful co-operation between public authorities and voluntary agencies' that Beveridge called for has yet to be fully realised – and to ensure civil society flourishes, it must properly represent all of society and be led accordingly.

Remember, it is these leaders in our civil society who decide how public services will be delivered. They decide what charities and NGOs will be supported.

They decide how unequal we want our society to be.

10

NATIONAL SECURITY

As long as I can remember, the armed forces have held a special connection with my family. It goes back to World War II when my grandfather provided catering services to troops in pre-Partition India and neighbouring Burma (now Myanmar).

My dad helped him and, much later, he and I would watch the BBC comedy series *It Ain't Half Hot, Mum* and he would tell me that the 'charwallah' character was based on someone like him.

Independence and Partition devastated my family, as it did millions of others, but my father never lost his affection for the British armed forces. So much so that when the opportunity arose to provide catering services again in the late 1950s, only this time in Cyprus, off he went leaving his young family in Pakistan so he could earn enough to support them.

Unfortunately, he ended up getting ripped off by a Brit in Cyprus and lost a sizeable amount of money. But my dad wasn't going to kiss goodbye to his life savings without a fight, so he made his way to the UK to track down the thief who'd tricked him.

I never did ask how he recovered his money. But once justice had prevailed, his eyes were opened to the opportunities that the

UK offered. He subsequently brought his young family over and a year later I was born.

However, working in a factory never really appealed to him and as soon as the Troubles broke out in Northern Ireland at the end of the 1960s, he was off to Belfast, providing catering services to the British troops there.

There was, as I recall, a process of tendering for catering contracts with each individual regiment rather than the army centrally. Tendering itself was an interesting process and the key decision-maker that determined who got the contract was the Regimental Quartermaster (RQM). I will never forget (as a 10-year-old) travelling south to an army base in a van with my dad and one of his cousins to see one RQM, with a large Persian carpet in the back.

I remember waking up at the end of the drive to witness his cousin throwing up at the side of the road because of travel sickness, which then set me off too. The RQM, I subsequently learned, had requested the carpet in order to agree to the contract. Now, in later life I would think he was corrupt, but at the time such thoughts didn't enter my mind.

My family, led by dad and my older brothers, spent several years going back and forth to Northern Ireland for months at a time working all the hours God gave them to earn a few pennies on each cup of tea or sandwich.

In 1974, one of my family members, Noor Baz Khan, working alongside my dad, was collecting supplies from a cash-and-carry to restock the shop. He had an even younger member of my family with him when suddenly their van was pulled over by masked men and both of them were bundled into the other van. Noor was shot in the face at point blank range and the Republican Terrorists told the other this was a message to my father that they must all leave Northern Ireland immediately and stop working with the British armed forces.

I remember seeing Noor's body at his funeral and witnessed my father's tears and, probably, his guilt. My father's response, though, was to stay working with the British in Northern Ireland for another decade until the Army's own catering company, the NAAFI, stopped issuing contracts. The IRA didn't defeat him, the British Army's own bureaucrats did that.

In all the years my dad worked alongside the military, he never complained about being treated differently because of his colour. However, in later life, he told me of hundreds of occasions when he and others were racially abused by those he was serving. 'It was part of the job,' he said with a shrug. He never met a non-white senior officer despite having worked with dozens of regiments. In fact, back then he rarely met a non-white soldier at all.

That, however, changed in the 1970s and he conceded that senior officers too were treated with disdain by their white colleagues. The words 'paki' and 'nigger' were commonplace in the mess rooms and canteens, so much so that his staff and black soldiers answered each time they were addressed using them. You have to remember that, at the time, the media openly used these words, especially in comedy, so I cannot blame these brave men and women.

However, despite these words subsequently disappearing from the media and common usage, racism in the armed forces has not gone away.

In 2021, a Freedom of Information request to the Ministry of Justice found that only 0.4 per cent of senior officers in the British Army are black. And, in recent years, there have been countless examples of egregious cases of racism in the British Army. Some 25 years since the 1998 Strategic Defence Review called for greater integration and representation in the army, every year more and more stories surface of deep-rooted prejudice against soldiers of colour.

Whether it's serving soldiers being put on trial for neo-Nazi activity, a black poster girl for a recruitment campaign being abused on social media by her fellow soldiers, or soldiers of colour being repeatedly subject to bullying and racist language, it's become common knowledge that the military is not doing enough to tackle racism.

My dad's experience had highlighted an uncomfortable truth that the army have been avoiding for decades – that despite their long service to Britain, and courage and commitment, people of colour are simply not valued. We all saw the appalling treatment of the Gurkhas, who were left to live in poverty. Despite having fought for our country for generations and won multiple Victoria Crosses – the highest award given to the military for the ultimate act of bravery and selflessness – they were cruelly denied the right to settle in the UK.

But it's not just major scandals like this that we're aware of nowadays. For years, a casual and cruel racism operating on a daily basis in the military was ignored. Not anymore though. Media reporting has exposed a dangerous faultline in the military, where stories of black soldiers being put in overflow dorms to separate them from white soldiers and news of ethnic minority soldiers being subject to regular comments such as 'people like you' and 'you people from the colonies' are more frequent.

Countless examples of this toxic culture have been heard at tribunals, leaked WhatsApp messages and from whistleblower testimony. Some, like the social media posts on a British army gossip forum that were exposed following the killing of a 21-year-old Kenyan woman by a British soldier at a training base in Kenya, are too sickening to print.

This horrific example refers to Agnes Wanjiru, who was last seen leaving a bar in Kenya with two soldiers in 2012. Her body was found two months later in a sceptic tank in Nanyuki, where the British army has a permanent training support base. Soldiers joked about her death on social media forums and, despite an inquest ruling that Wanjiru was 'murdered by British soldiers', no action has been taken. Such indifference and lack of accountability perfectly illustrates how the lives of people of colour are valued by the army.

Sadly, Wanjiru's tragic story is just one of countless examples of toxic racism that has brought shame on the army in recent years. In 2019, the service complaints ombudsman for the armed forces admitted that 'Incidents of racism are occurring with increasing and depressing frequency' and the Defence Secretary, Ben Wallace, admitted that the Ministry of Defence's record on discrimination against black and minority ethnic personnel was 'woeful'.

He went on to tell Parliament's in-house publication, the *House Magazine*, that the army's failure to tackle racism was cutting off a critical supply of talent.

'By not having more BAME personnel, not having more women, we are losing the opportunity to have some great talent. It's really, really important that this is stopped, crushed, got rid of, and we have to double our efforts.'

This point has since been further underlined by the head of the armed forces. In Admiral Tony Radakin's first speech after being appointed to the role, he warned that if the army failed to reflect the diverse nation it serves, then, 'quite simply we risk looking ridiculous'.

Firmly rejecting the idea that diversity was about 'wokeness', he argued that the failure to increase diversity was a source of shame.

'It is about woefulness,' he explained. 'The woefulness of too few women. The woefulness of not reflecting the ethnic, religious and cognitive diversity of our nation.'

That such grand statements from respected military leaders have yet to properly overturn a toxic culture of racism in the ranks shows just how stubbornly this is resisted in the army.

However, the same cannot be said of Britain's domestic counter intelligence and security agency.

Like the army, GCHQ similarly has a history of racism. The historian, John Ferris, revealed that the spy agency had a colour bar on employees for nearly three decades, with a ban on hiring non-white staff in place from the 1950s to 1980.

Much has changed in recent years, though. My role as a senior prosecutor, particularly when I was Chief Prosecutor, meant that I had the privilege of dealing with some of the most serious cases in the land. So it will be no surprise that I frequently engaged with the security services, particularly the internal service MI5, or 'box' as we called it.

For obvious reasons I cannot either name the cases or the members of our intelligence services that I engaged with. Secret is as secret does.

It has to be said, however, that these brave men and women keep us safe day in and day out by putting themselves in dangerous situations with some very scary people. They do so without recognition, such is the nature of their work.

I noticed that in the early years of the twenty-first century, I did not come across any officer who was a person of colour and certainly not at senior levels. I also noticed how this changed during the lifetime of my prosecutorial career. More and more black, Asian and minority ethnic people began to represent the security services, presumably as both the country and the threat changed. It appeared to me that the security services quickly understood that their endeavours would be more successful if they better reflected the diversity of the population.

With the increased threat from radicalised individuals, having officers that both understood the communities they hid in and also being able to blend in without sticking out, was absolutely necessary. They didn't make a song and dance about it, they just changed their recruitment strategy and did it.

It must be said that 99.9 per cent of people from these communities detest what criminals are doing and so it was no surprise when the heads of the security services told us that the vast majority of their intelligence was volunteered directly from these communities. That can only be done by building trusting relationships and that is significantly easier if the officer knows the community.

I saw closehand our security services slowly becoming more diverse. And not just in recruiting people of colour. They have actively recruited more women and embraced neurodiversity and the LGBT+ community. So much so that nowadays they are very open about this drive and under the diversity and inclusion section on GCHQ's website, it states: 'We're confident we can succeed because with the right mix of minds anything is possible.' This didn't happen overnight, though, and the cultural change was brought about through successive MI6 Chiefs beginning to emphasise the value of intellectual and cultural diversity in approaching the many challenges they face.

When I spoke to a security source, who understandably wished to remain anonymous, to learn more about this change, he said successive Chiefs of MI6 came to emphasise the value of intellectual and cultural diversity and this was heavily driven by Sir Alex Younger in his period as Chief. The move towards diversity in all the security services, he added, arose from both principle and practice.

'The principle was driven by a genuine desire tinged with anxiety, for the services to reflect society as a whole, and to ensure that nobody in their employment was marginalised by their sexuality or race,' he explained. 'MI6's drive for increased diversity came at a time when major public and private sector organisations were seeking determinately (and were required by law) to ensure that characteristics protected by law were met within their organisations. So they tried to develop and enhance their recruitment efforts and improve access for sectors of the community which would not automatically have been associated with their work.'

However, this was not without problems as it posed difficulties in the recruitment process.

'MI6 receives very large numbers of expressions of interest,' he noted, 'and if they are to achieve diversity, the initial phases of recruitment are performed via online processes. Creating algorithms which contain no relics of old-fashioned tropes is a sophisticated Human Resources task.'

And if the principled drive to widen the diversity meant old practices needed shaking up, the practical reasons meant conventional wisdom no longer held.

'In practical terms, the wisdom of MI6 encouraging and embracing diversity becomes self-evident when one examines the backgrounds of terrorists and other targets of their work. The reduction and detection of terrorism in and against our country, at least where the terrorists profess Islamist theology, requires staff who speak and write Arabic languages fluently, preferably learned naturally as small children. The increased cosmopolitan nature of the UK, including as it does many whose families have come to the country from Central and Eastern Europe (including Russia), also provides a broader cohort of potential staff. In recognition of this, historic impediments to joining the agencies for people whose families are from outside the UK have been diluted.'

My source concluded that Parliament's Intelligence and Security Committee has been keeping a close eye on these developments. But all the signs indicate that a more diverse pool of staff provides greater effectiveness and is fast becoming business critical.

Nowadays, our intelligence services are not only confident about flaunting their commitment to diversity – they actively boast about it as one of the greatest strengths of the West.

'Diversity of thought and speaking truth to power are some of our greatest strengths,' argues the head of GCHQ, Sir Jeremy Fleming. 'Not just in GCHQ but as a Western coalition. It helps us to refine our decision-making, challenge our assumptions and – from an intelligence perspective – use the truth to counter disinformation.'

It's an admirable thought. Yet, unlike the rhetoric of Radakin and Wallace, Fleming's words resonate strongly because they are reflected in his organisation. Because while diversity still appears something that our armed forces are culturally uncomfortable with – and, in the most extreme cases, genuinely ashamed of – it's something our intelligence services are rightly proud of.

There have been hundreds of terrorist convictions in the UK since 9/11 and multiple late-stage terrorist plots foiled by our intelligence services. For this, we owe an enormous gratitude to brave men and women– but ultimately we should give thanks to diversity.

It's now deeply understood across Britain's biggest spy agency that diversity is an incredibly powerful weapon that gives us a vital edge and saves lives. How long can it be then before the first person of colour takes charge at GCHQ?

11

FAILING UP IS NO WAY TO LEVEL UP

There comes a point in anyone's career when we all encounter Gavin.

Not necessarily the Gavin I'm thinking of, but you will know the type. I'm sure you will have seen them in your workplace. They're brash, confident and stunningly mediocre. But they always fail up. No matter how hopeless they are, how poorly they perform or how dismal their track record is, they always seem to get promoted and continue to move on to bigger and better things.

Of course, the Gavin I'm thinking of is the former Cabinet Minister, Gavin Williamson MP. But it could equally be any number of mediocre chief executives, senior managers or associates who are awarded undeserving bonuses, given bigger and better paid jobs or made a partner in the firm.

In recent years, there's a growing awareness of how 'Gavins' are inveigling their way into seats at the top table in every industry. You'll see their rictus grin on annual reports and occasionally hear them babbling away on your radio, but you'll struggle to find much evidence of the value they deliver. In the banking sector they're the kind that lost the taxpayer billions of pounds by not understanding how their own complicated financial instruments worked. In politics they're ubiquitous and barely a week passes without a minister claiming not to understand how the Dover–Calais crossing impacts British trade or somehow confusing Daniel Radcliffe with Marcus Rashford. While, in education, they're busy changing their titles from Vice Chancellor to President to try and justify salaries that are more than three times what the Prime Minister earns.

Williamson arguably remains the best recent example of this, though largely because his baffling ascent has been very public. We've all seen how as Defence Minister and then Education Secretary he presided over all sorts of debacles. From being sacked for leaking information from a meeting of the National Security Council, to the 2020 A-levels fiasco that saw pupils from disadvantaged backgrounds get their results downgraded, he has continually demonstrated the opposite Midas touch.

Many of his colleagues didn't think much of him either. Former Foreign Office Minister Alan Duncan famously said of Williamson when he was made Defence Minister that this 'was the most extraordinary Cabinet appointment I can think of'.

Duncan didn't hold back on why he'd reached this conclusion.

'He is ludicrously unqualified for the heavyweight job of Defence Secretary, having never run anything. His experience amounts to having been a fireplace salesman, then bag-carrier for two PMs, then chief whip for a year. What on earth was the PM thinking?'

Despite failing in every position he held in Government and leaving a trail of chaos in his wake, Williamson was continually promoted into bigger and better jobs. And to cap it all, when his position as Education Secretary became totally untenable and he had to be removed from the post, having lost the confidence of parents, teachers and trade unions, the Prime Minister rewarded him with a knighthood.

To begin to understand what the Prime Minister or any other decision-maker is thinking when promoting mediocre people to undeserving positions, it's worth examining what social psychologists call the Dunning-Kruger effect.

Named after American psychologists David Dunning and Justin Kruger, it refers to a cognitive bias where people who are incompetent at something are unable to recognise their incompetence. This lack of self-awareness about their limitations is only one part of the package, though. The Dunning-Kruger effect also vastly inflates people's perceived ability and sees them possessing a bullet-proof confidence and unshakeable belief that they are highly competent, when all the evidence suggests otherwise.

This phenomenon was launched following Dunning and Kruger's 1999 paper, 'Unskilled and Unaware of It: How Difficulties in Recognising One's Own Incompetence Lead to Inflated Self-Assessments'. Subsequent examples of the bias have been demonstrated in every industry.

Of course, we are all susceptible to thinking we know more about something than we actually do. But for those operating at the extreme end of the Dunning-Kruger effect, their overbearing confidence and inflated sense of their abilities can be all too attractive to hiring managers.

In short, those who stride into a room exuding confidence, charisma and appearing to be in full control of their brief tend to be seen as a better fit for senior roles.

And, as the respected journalist, Zulekha Nathoo, notes: 'Once an individual is promoted, they become more visible to management, recruiters and other leaders; experience on a resumé begins to hold more value than actual performance outcome. And, perhaps most importantly, once an employee is promoted, bosses become invested in that person's success because it becomes a reflection of their own judgement. Failures are downplayed and losses are spun into wins.'

But if the Dunning-Kruger effect is one clear example of how bias is shown in creating a culture of mediocre leadership, another important bias is that of cultural matching.

Research in the *American Sociological Review* has shown that employers seek candidates who are culturally similar to themselves, and that concerns about shared culture often overrule concerns about productivity. Neuropsychologists also use the term 'affinity bias' to show how we unconsciously gravitate towards people like ourselves in appearance, beliefs and background.

These factors, along with the unconscious bias we all suffer from to some degree in terms of prejudice absorbed from our experiences and upbringing, make a mockery of the much vaunted ideal of meritocracy.

Indeed, many argue that affinity bias turns meritocracy into a 'mirrorocracy', where decision-makers are more concerned about excluding people who are different to them or perceived as a threat rather than rewarding and promoting talent. There are many theorists now making a compelling case that meritocracy is bogus, arguing that merit has little to do with the advancement of so many of our leaders. The American philosopher, Michael Sandel, for example, calls meritocracy a 'myth, a distant promise that has yet to be redeemed'.

He argues that the fabled level playing field is an illusion and the professional classes have long figured out how to game the system and pass on advantages to their children, converting 'meritocracy into a hereditary aristocracy'.

In the course of researching this book I've seen countless examples of how the meritocratic assumptions that underpin our political discourse are a nonsense. When nearly one in three colleges from our most prestigious university fail to admit a single black British A-level student, as Oxford University did in 2015, then it's clear that something is wrong. We are not living in an age of merit when research shows that black graduates end up with notably worse economic outcomes than white classmates who entered university with similar qualifications and backgrounds. From business, to sports and film and TV to religion, I've seen examples of a system that slams doors on people of colour and pulls up the ladder of opportunity.

But if there's one incident that best encapsulates how Britain has lost its moorings to any semblance of a meritocracy, it's necessary to return to Sir Gavin and the A-levels fiasco he presided over in the summer of 2020.

Let's forget for a moment that, in a poor attempt to hide his unsuitability for the job as Education Secretary, Williamson had previously told journalists he couldn't remember what A-level grades he achieved.

Instead, let's examine the nightmare that unfolded for many young people when they received their A-level results in lockdown, an experience that, unlike Williamson, they won't forget. Students had long known that their results would be determined differently in 2020, as Williamson had declared that exams would have to be cancelled. So an algorithm was created by exams regulator Ofqual, supported by ministers, to determine results.

When the results were finally issued on 13 August, it quickly became apparent that they were deeply flawed and riddled with bias: 40 per cent of grades were downgraded, hitting disadvantaged students the hardest. While private schools saw the largest spike in A* grades, pupils in lower socio-economic backgrounds were left in tears as their results were adjusted downwards. As Chair of Hopwood Hall College, I shared their anger, as I see all the time how hard young people work to build a better future.

Despite Williamson eventually apologising after digging his heels in and promising 'no U-turn, no change' before he blamed the algorithm and re-issued grades, the damage had already been done. The algorithm was dropped but subsequent stories of private schools 'gaming the system' to massively inflate the proportion of students achieving A* grades has shown a rigged system masquerading as a meritocracy.

It was one, albeit highly symbolic, moment in a pandemic that has seen inequalities and unfairness become more deeply embodied and entrenched.

All of this makes it even more puzzling why our leaders have long ignored these widening fault lines and trumpeted meritocracy as a guiding British virtue.

Margaret Thatcher was the first Prime Minister I can remember to evoke meritocracy by telling the nation that 'whatever your background, you have a chance to climb to the top'. Years later I remember John Major echoing the same sentiment, promising a 'classless society'. Then Tony Blair never stopped talking about it. 'The Britain of the elite is over, the new Britain is a meritocracy,' he said in 1997. David Cameron had a vision of 'aspirational meritocracy' and Theresa May famously promised to make Britain the 'world's great meritocracy'. Boris Johnson continued in this vein, promising to 'spread opportunity to every corner of the UK'.

But however well-intentioned these aims were, they were all guilty of wishful thinking and ignoring the rigged system that needs dismantling first.

If we're ever to realise a Britain where all talents can rise, we need to stop recruiting solely from privileged and limited pools of Oxbridge talent, recognise the dangers of affinity bias and stop rewarding failure.

There are far too many examples of white middle-aged leaders elevated to positions of power that simply don't reflect their abilities and are entirely undeserved. The former CEO of the Royal Bank of Scotland, Fred Goodwin, the Chairman of the Co-operative Bank, Paul Flowers, and England football manager Sam Allardyce are some examples that we all know about. But there are many more in companies, institutions and other organisations that are not so well known.

And yet you will struggle to find examples in Britain of ethnic minority leaders who are allowed to continually fail upwards. On the contrary, people of colour who attain leadership positions frequently find their performance judged much more harshly than white leaders.

Look at black football managers, for example. Incredibly, there have only been 10 in the history of the Premier League, and the first black British manager in the top flight was Paul Ince, who took charge of Blackburn Rovers in 2008. He lasted just 21 games. Then consider Darren Moore, who took charge of West Bromwich Albion in April 2018, with the club firmly rooted at the bottom of the Premier League with a month of the season remaining. He had an immediate impact and the club went undefeated in April, including a victory away at Manchester United. Moore won the Premier League manager of the month award but it wasn't enough to stop West Brom being relegated.

The following season, with the club well positioned to return to the Premier League, Moore was sacked, prompting an outpouring of outrage. Another example is that of John Barnes. He was sacked after just eight months at Celtic and has subsequently been outspoken on why it's much harder to succeed as a black manager.

'If they are bad, white managers lose their jobs. Lose their jobs, get another job, lose their jobs, get another job,' he argued. 'Or they are given longer to fail.'

On his time at Celtic, he said from early on he could feel that too many felt he didn't fit in there and wanted him to fail.

'In the first 13 games we won 11, lost one and drew one,' he recalled. 'I was getting so much criticism by people who thought I shouldn't have been there that I knew it wasn't going to last. Even when we were doing OK. I said as soon as we go through a sticky patch, I'm going to be gone.'

Barnes's views are certainly not sour grapes, as there are plenty of examples of celebrated white managers who failed in their first jobs, only to be given bigger and better opportunities elsewhere. None of the black managers mentioned here have subsequently received high-profile job offers. Their first failure saw them condemned as damaged goods.

Multiple trophy winner Antonio Conte, on the other hand, was sacked from his first job as manager of Arezzo with the club incredibly on -1 points! The former Tottenham boss, Harry Redknapp, lost 9-0 on his managerial debut, and former England manager, Sam Allardyce, who was always in the frame whenever a vacancy came up was sacked from his first managerial stint at West Brom after losing to non-league Woking. I do wonder whether all of these managers would have been able to go on to achieve later success had they been black.

Another troubling trend is that women and people of colour who are appointed as leaders are frequently given the opportunity only in difficult times. Left isolated and set up to fail, this is known as the 'glass cliff' phenomenon. Researchers at the University of Exeter examined the appointments of women to the boards of FTSE 100 companies and found that when companies were performing poorly, women were appointed. The subtle discrimination is that they were set up to fail, and research has similarly shown the same correlation with ethnic minorities being offered precarious leadership positions in politics, sport and business.

'In times of crisis, companies don't want to risk the loss of who they believe to be their most valuable, high-potential talent – white men,' explains the Chief Executive of Pinsight and author Martin Lanik. 'In tough times, they are more likely to sacrifice employees who they perceive as less valued and more dispensable – women and racial minorities.'

All of these trends, however, from affinity bias and the Dunning-Kruger effect, to the glass cliff phenomenon, have long been downplayed by politicians who want us to believe that the old class divisions and barriers have been swept away by a rising tide of meritocracy.

Admittedly, a few, like former Education Secretary Justine Greening, have argued that companies should adopt name blind or contextual recruitment processes, which seek to eliminate barriers faced by people because of their background. But, for the most part, there remains a cosy consensus around the idea that our system provides everyone an equal opportunity by giving out what we are able to put in, through people's innate ability or hard work.

Much of this consensus has, naturally, been created by those who are beneficiaries of an old boys' network of privilege, which still dominates the most influential positions across leading British organisations.

Reports like *Elitist Britain*, by the Sutton Trust and Social Mobility Commission, for example, show just how prevalent this is. While only 7 per cent of British people are privately educated, a tiny network of private schools wields enormous influence in determining who runs the country.

Some 65 per cent of senior judges, 59 per cent of civil service permanent secretaries, 52 per cent of Foreign and Commonwealth diplomats, 57 per cent of the House of Lords and over 50 per cent of the Government's cabinet are privately educated. A study by the London School of Economics has also found that alumni from the UK's nine leading public schools are 94 times more likely to reach the elite than those who attended non-fee paying schools. These so-called Clarendon schools produce nearly 10 per cent of all *Who's Who* entrants despite traditionally educating just 0.15 per cent of the population.

Similarly, Britain's media, also known as the Fourth Estate, possesses large numbers of privately educated people. Of the 100 most influential news editors and broadcasters, 43 per cent went to fee-paying schools. Likewise, 44 per cent of newspaper columnists were privately educated. There is a vast body of research demonstrating how strong this network of privilege is, and a further study by the EHRC in 2016 found that nearly a third of the UK's biggest companies largely rely on personal networks to identify new board members.

Is it any wonder then that those at the top who benefit from this exclusive network of privilege are bound to doggedly defend it? Should we be surprised that a privately educated elite at the heart of Britain's political class are reluctant to disavow their inheritance?

Toby Young is one of the best examples of this. The journalist and columnist who was appointed by Government to its higher education watchdog in 2018, has spent a large part of his career railing against diversity, calling for the Equality Act to be repealed and bemoaning that there's something 'ghastly' about schools having to include children in wheelchairs. And yet, while Young is happy to insist that hiring decisions should be based on what he thinks is likely to be most successful for society, he's less keen on including his own privilege in these arguments.

Young admits having got into Oxford University on a technicality after failing to achieve the grades he needed. As he wrote in the pages of the *Spectator*, having received both a rejection letter and a letter of acceptance addressed to the wrong person, his father, Baron Young of Dartington (a sociologist who – and this is where irony explodes – first coined the term meritocracy), rang up the admissions office at Brasenose College and he was subsequently offered a place.

The main beneficiaries of this meritocracy illusion will, as Michael Sandel pithily observes, always wish to perpetuate it.

'In an unequal society, those who land on top want to believe their success is morally justified,' he argues. 'In a meritocratic society, this means the winners must believe they have earned their success through their own talent and hard work.'

It is, however, more than just self-aggrandising from our political leaders that's keeping the meritocracy consensus intact. The new flat earthers loudly cheerleading the outdated ideals of meritocracy are rooted in an enduring mythology that's defined politics for centuries.

This is, of course, the bootstrap myth, which is the idea that all people, regardless of how poor or difficult their upbringing, can 'pull themselves up by their bootstraps' to attain wealth and high office. The problem is that the majority of politicians appropriating this myth for their own ends have no such backstory and conveniently ignore the privileges that benefit them. They are, in the words of Sandel again, seeking to borrow the 'lustre of merit'.

Bootstrapping has become a powerful pillar of Western political mythology, though, and challenging this fallacy frequently provokes strong reactions. Despite the fact that all the evidence shows that social mobility in Britain is in absolute decline, the meritocrats will accuse you of siding with the dead hand of the state and standing against individual liberty.

This grandstanding entirely misses the point about a system that deliberately blocks individual talent because it's biased towards a small coterie of people who look the same and have similar experiences. But the bootstrapping argument is continually advanced. One of the best ripostes I can recall to this view, though, was from Bill Clinton's Democratic National Convention speech in 2012.

To laughter in the room, as he took on the narrative that anyone who amounts to anything is completely self-made, he said, 'every politician wants every voter to believe he was born in a log cabin he built himself . . . it ain't so.'

But puncturing Republican politicians' egos is one thing. Changing a deep-seated consensus around meritocracy in Britain is a wholly different challenge.

To do this, Britain needs to take a different approach, rethink our values and re-examine what modern British culture means.

And if all talents genuinely have an opportunity to shine and progress then we need to ask why we continually revert to a certain limited stereotype when we think of who is suitable for leadership.

It's no secret that people form images of what leadership or achievement look like from an early age, and much of this is determined by education and popular culture. And while we may have moved on from the backwards depiction of black people in films like *Zulu* and *Gone with the Wind*, as the likes of Disney and Netflix have put positive diversity at the heart of their filmmaking, our education system is still horribly guilty of ignoring the achievements of people of colour.

Too often, children are only taught about the achievements of white inventors, scientists, leaders and explorers. Everyone knows Thomas Edison invented the light bulb, right? But most don't know how the African American inventor, Lewis Latimer, paved the way for this discovery.

Latimer had already helped Alexander Graham Bell patent the telephone in 1876 before he drew the first electric light blueprints and invented and patented a process for making carbon filaments for lightbulbs. He would go on to improve Edison's invention (which lasted less than 15 hours) by finding a way to prevent the carbon from breaking and subsequently creating a longer lasting bulb that was cheaper and much more efficient.

There are, of course, many other great black inventors, explorers and fascinating figures that no one is ever taught about at school. Like Septimius Severus, the first black Roman Emperor, the writer Ignatius Sancho, who was the first black person to vote in parliamentary elections in Britain, the mathematician Gladys West, who helped invent the GPS system, Mae Carol Jemison, the first African American woman to travel in space, the soprano Camilla Williams, who was the first black person to have a major role with the Vienna State Opera, and Garrett Morgan, who invented the traffic light and the gas mask, which saved the lives of millions of soldiers and firefighters.

Morgan's story is harrowing and inspiring in equal measure. His live-saving invention nearly failed to reach the market because racism was so rife, preventing people from buying his breathing device. The only way Morgan could get round this was to hire a white actor in 1914 to pose as the inventor. Only then was he able to sell his breathing device, which became the prototype for gas masks worn by soldiers during World War I.

Once you take a wider trawl through history, you'll see it's filled with people of colour doing amazing things that kids today hardly know anything about. Do they know about great towering black and Asian public intellectuals and writers? Do they know figures like Al Zahrawi, the father of operative surgery, or that Muslims invented coffee, hospitals and university?

Probably not, but they certainly know of rappers killed in drive-by shootings, famous gangbangers and plenty of racial stereotypes from Muslim terrorists to black criminals. How could they not when our media sears these negative depictions into our minds every day?

None of which is likely to instil young people of colour with the confidence to aspire to greater things and start to think of themselves as future leaders.

As I write this, the professional footballer Troy Deeney has launched a campaign for black experiences to be taught in class. He's written to the Education Secretary and commissioned research by YouGov, which shows that 54 per cent of teachers believe the school system or national curriculum has a racial bias, rising to 93 per cent among minority ethnic teachers.

It's a strong campaign, but what struck me most were his own reflections on the schooling he received as a youngster.

'My only experience of black history or black culture was through the food or music I experienced at home, whilst at school I felt detached,' he said. 'Not only was I not taught about positive role models who looked like me, I was even told by one teacher that I'd be dead by the time I was 25.'

Such experiences not only alienate and disempower people of colour but also start to create a mindset that will subconsciously always see high achievers and leaders as white.

Beginning to untangle this toxic skein of prejudice and bias is not going to happen overnight. And it will not only require an honest reappraisal of every stage on the pathway to achievement – from schooling to hiring to boardroom composition. It will also require a similarly sober examination of the capability of leaders running our country.

And I'm afraid the tough conclusion this will inevitably reach is that we currently have a paucity of talent at the top of our key institutions.

In the decade after the financial crisis of 2008, Britain's economic efficiency fell to its worst level in 250 years, and our productivity has been flatlining ever since. But when debate focuses on our productivity crisis, which continues to lag behind our G7 peers, talk always turns to transport networks, capital investment and skills. These are, of course, all incredibly important but very little debate is ever given over to leadership.

When it does, we will have to face up to the fact that we're living in an age of failing leadership.

Wherever we look, for many years now, there has been no hiding from it. You can see it in the bullying, vanity and greed of former Arcadia boss, Sir Philip Green, in the colossal failures of the Carillion collapse and the litany of lies and scandals at the heart of our Government.

Some would argue this deterioration began with a late twenti-eth-century wave of so-called experts who ushered in the idea that to manage an organisation you didn't need to know what that organisation was doing. This represented a significant departure in leadership theory. While previous leaders often worked their way to the top from the shop floor and had a deep knowledge of the company, this new model of leadership placed no emphasis on 'domain knowledge' and bet the house on management wizardry.

Unfortunately, no amount of snake oil can help organisations escape from hard realities at the coalface. A deeply disconnected leadership has resulted in countless examples of failure because it simply didn't understand the reality it operated in.

You can see this in the Royal Bank of Scotland accountant-turned-banker Fred Goodwin, whose failure to understand sub-prime problems cost the taxpayer billions. And it's there again in the Stafford Hospital scandal, where staffing levels were cut to a point where 'nurses were immune to the sound of pain'. In both cases, decision-making at the top was rendered useless by a lack of domain knowledge.

And yet, when such failures occur, for all the handwringing and recriminations, little changes. A new charlatanism has become normalised and our leadership reflects this.

It's why it became normal to refer to our former Transport Minister as Chris 'failing' Grayling on account of his multiple cock-ups, such as awarding a contract to a company with no ferries to charter ferries in a no-Brexit scenario. It's also why, despite national outrage, the Government were somehow able to appoint Tory Peer Dido Harding first as Chair of the powerful hospital regulator NHS Improvement and then put her in charge of the Test and Trace programme.

Harding, or Baroness Harding of Winscombe to give her full title, has a history of failing upwards. As Chief Executive of telecoms group TalkTalk, she was handed record fines by Ofcom for overbilling and saw the company's shares lose two thirds of their value.

Her appointment to NHS Improvement was resisted by a Commons Select Committee for her 'complete lack of experience' in healthcare. And as head of the Test and Trace programme she has spent £37 billion on what was slammed as 'the most wasteful and inept public spending programme of all time'.

When leadership inspires it can be genuinely transformative. The best leaders inspire those around them to think, do and be better. Bad leaders, on the other hand, make everyone worse. They pull us down to their level and ensure that mediocrity becomes the accepted standard.

This has become the hallmark of bog-standard Britannia.

We've shrunk and corrupted the notion of leadership so much that all that's left is an inept fail-upwards chumocracy.

You can see this is the billions of pounds of 'crony contracts' that were awarded during the pandemic by the Government to Tory donors and favoured associates. And you can see it play out on a daily basis in our major institutions. Just look at the debacle in the Metropolitan Police where Police Commissioner Cressida Dick oversaw a culture of incompetence and cover-up. Presiding over incidents such as the rape and murder of Sarah Everard by a serving Metropolitan Police officer, to the murder of Daniel Morgan, which saw an independent report describe the Met as 'institutionally corrupt', she led the force through a shameful period where officers were exposed for being sexist, homophobic and racist.

And yet, despite a catalogue of failings, it was reported that she was offered a two-year extension to her contract because the Home Secretary had decided there was no one suitable to replace her.

This in itself perfectly encapsulates the leadership problems dogging our institutions. A tiny talent pool of mediocrity and a failing leader overseeing a massive loss of public confidence in policing who cannot be replaced because all the other leaders are privately deemed to be equally bad or worse. What does this say about leadership in Britain? How can we possibly say we're harnessing all the talent in our country when Government contracts and senior positions are awarded on the basis of what school you went to, whether you're in a minister's WhatsApp group or whether you have personal ties to those doing the appointing?

Britain has had enough of unaccountable fail-ups and leadership stitch-ups. Much of our nation's leadership doctrine has been exposed as hollow, and too many of our most cherished institutions are haemorrhaging confidence because of bad leadership.

Yet there is a new generation of hungry, smart and immensely capable leaders in waiting. They're in every community, every workplace and they've been overlooked for too long.

It's time they were given their chance.

12

NO MORE TUNNEL VISION

I can remember exactly where I was when the MacPherson Report into the circumstances following the murder of Stephen Lawrence was published. It was 1999 and I was restlessly pacing the CPS headquarters in Ludgate Hill in the shadow of Saint Paul's Cathedral. I was awaiting my copy and eager to know what it was going to conclude after nearly two years of sometimes depressing evidence of incompetence and inaction.

And there it was in black and white.

The police investigation was beset by institutional racism. I knew it to be true, but just didn't expect a statutory inquiry report to say it so starkly.

What followed was a spate of institutions, including my own, declaring with almost indecent haste that, we too, were institutionally racist. It's difficult to exaggerate the impact it had on race inequality in the UK. Though, with hindsight, I came to realise that institutions were keen to make the announcement so as to bizarrely take the attention away from them and let it focus on those that were dragging their heels. 'Look at them now, not us.'

Fast forward two decades and the worldwide 'Black Lives Matter' protests following the murder of George Floyd in the United States saw the UK Government respond with a report from the Commission on Race and Ethnic Disparities chaired by Tony Sewell. Published in March 2021, this had significant implications for racial equality in our country, and came in for a substantial amount of criticism, including from me.

It was meant to take the temperature of racial inequality but, in my view, despite some interesting contributions, failed to reflect the reality of racism experienced by people of colour. It looked at four key areas: education and training; employment; fairness at work and enterprise; crime, policing and health. It had access to cabinet office data and analysts, and all the reports previously produced going back over four decades.

The headlines were, however, taken up by statements within the report. Most notably its controversial assurance that, 'put simply, we no longer see a Britain where the system is deliberately rigged against ethnic minorities. The impediments and disparities do exist, they are varied, and ironically very few of them are directly to do with racism. Too often, racism is the catch all explanation and can be implicitly accepted rather than explicitly examined. The evidence shows that geography, family influence, socio-economic background, culture and religion have more significant impact on life chances than racism.' This was inevitably shortened to, 'there is no institutional or structural racism'.

The report argued that the term 'institutional racism' was 'devalued through linguistic inflation', and should only be used if you can prove systemic racism. But, curiously, not when acts are 'well-meaning'. So if there are individual failures, which are not designed or deliberate, then it's not an institutional problem. The Windrush scandal, which led to the resignation of the Home Secretary, Amber Rudd, following the unlawful deportation of black Britons who had arrived here legally as children, was one such example of a 'not deliberately targeted' policy – though few would agree.

I learnt through my legal career, particularly as an advocate, that if you ask leading questions you get the answers you want. If you ask certain witnesses their views but ignore others, then you get the evidence you want. It's called 'tunnel vision' in investigations and it means that you either don't hear contrary views or you give them insufficient weight. It is at the heart of every miscarriage of justice I know.

Think about the biggest miscarriage of justice in recent years: the Post Office Horizon scandal, which led to the wrongful prosecution and convictions of 700 law-abiding postmasters because an IT system said monies were missing when they weren't. During their trials, nobody listened to their complaints that 'the system is faulty', and juries said they were lying. They told the truth, but the systems failures were covered up.

I'm not saying that that the Sewell Report was a 'cover-up'; it just didn't ask the right questions of the right people. Its conclusions stood in contrast to the experiences of people of colour and it didn't sit comfortably with mounting evidence of systemic prejudice. It's right to recognise the complex interplay of race with other factors – but that certainly doesn't mean that race didn't play a big part. It's easier to prove that poverty plays a part if you are, say, from a broken home. But how do you prove the racism when everybody denies it?

In the area I know best, crime and policing, the report completely sidelined the David Lammy Review of Criminal Justice, commissioned by a Conservative Prime Minister just four years earlier, which found overt discrimination in the system.

The Sewell Report set out differences between different ethnic groups and argued that it's possible to have 'racial disadvantage without racists'. Having said that, it offered no meaningful explanation.

Instead it doubled down on the view that, 'we need to look elsewhere than racism for the roots of that disadvantage'. Why?

Furthermore, it contended that 'racial disadvantage often overlaps with social class disadvantage', but rapidly moved on from social class to discuss, 'how some groups have transcended that disadvantage more swiftly than others'. Of course, it then focused on 'family structure' and 'cultural traditions' being the reasons for why Chinese or Indian children might progress faster than Pakistani or Bengali heritage children. Within a few pages, it nimbly shifted from asking questions about racism to essentially blaming the communities for not doing enough to unburden themselves of racial disadvantage!

Like many others, I found this hard to stomach. The report wraps itself up in a confused mess when discussing how some children from minorities out-perform white working-class boys in education (true) without recognising that white working-class men out-perform non-white people in terms of income, employment and social mobility (also true).

Reaching for ever more peculiar conclusions, its response to the fact that white applicants are more likely to get job interviews was to blame minorities for being too choosy about jobs. Choosy? People from minority communities are more likely than their white counterparts to be working in low- or minimum-wage jobs. Just take a look at those working in cleaning roles in public and private institutions, or those picking fruit, or those running takeaways and other less financially rewarding roles. It beggars belief that anyone should suggest they 'choose' these long hours for very little money.

The report also ignores the many studies that show how people with names like mine, Asian or African sounding, would have to send in twice as many CVs to even get an interview. If the interviewer can't even be bothered to interview you for a role, how difficult do you imagine it will be to get the job and progress within it?

On every page these glaring inconsistencies continued. Arguing that minorities don't really like apprenticeships, it failed to acknowledge that they are NOT underrepresented. I'm chair of an FE college with a large apprenticeship cohort which properly reflects the diverse nature of the community we serve, and we are not alone. The problem, if there is one, is the dearth of apprenticeships.

When criticism began to target these inconsistencies and highlight the falsehoods contained in the report, contributors started quickly distancing themselves from it. Unfortunately, this coincided with some right wing commentators using it to validate their own prejudices.

It was disappointing, but entirely predictable. More frustrating, however, was how wrong some of the data was. In the chapter on crime it states, 'Class B drug offences (cannabis etc) accounted for nearly half of all prosecutions of almost all ethnic groups.' As someone who has been prosecuting for a quarter of a century, this left me scratching my head. In fact, the figure is about 1 per cent! This bogus figure formed the basis of several news stories which implied that people of colour are too stoned to do any real work.

It failed to capture a sense of the scale or gravity of the problem on so many fronts, and suffice to say it didn't get a good reception, other than from commentators on the right who saw it as fuel for various campaigns against 'wokeness' or 'culture wars'. It was a determined effort to rewrite the narrative that was taking hold in Britain, with footballers 'taking the knee' and the anti-colonial heritage campaigns including attacks on statues of colonialists or slave readers. It was an undisguised attempt to energise a 'fightback' and the Commission was either deliberately complicit or extraordinarily naive.

Many others spotted this. The Runnymede Trust notes that, 'the people involved in the report had no real interest in discussing racism'. Deborah Gold, CEO of the National AIDS Trust, went further 'The Commission's conclusions ignore evidence, real experiences, and defy logic.' She added that, 'rather than being a neutral collection of evidence, the review was designed to get answers that negate the systemic impact of racism in the UK'.

Shelter, the housing and homelessness charity, used their public response to remind people that, 'people of colour are disproportionately affected by the housing emergency. Every eight minutes, a person who is black, Asian or from an ethnic minority community becomes homeless or is threatened with homelessness. People of colour are more likely to be homeless, live in deprived communities, and be living in poor quality housing.'

Charity after charity continued in this vein. So too did the biggest and most established advocacy groups, all publicly condemning the report and stating that people of colour are disproportionately impacted by the country's ills, and that structural racism underpins this.

Then, to prove gaslighting exists, the report's author Tony Sewell gave evidence before MPs and declared, 'We did find evidence of race-based discrimination', despite barely mentioning it in the report itself. 'We can be wise after the event,' he mused. Another Commission member, Keith Fraser, told the same committee of MPs, 'we know that institutional racism exists', even though their report denied it. I hope that they when they receive their knighthoods, damehoods or peerages, the Commission members get time to reflect on the damage they have done.

It felt like a pivotal moment, as the report disappeared into that notorious filing cabinet in Whitehall that's full of missed opportunities.

A year later, the Government eventually responded with their Inclusion Britain-report in which they agreed with virtually everything the Sewell Report said. But, in the hope that they might be seen as more reasonable and not draw such stinging criticism, it said things like, 'Of course, there is racism' and 'Of course there's a bigger picture'. We saw through this charade when the report they commissioned claimed to be looking at the bigger picture.

It's only fair to look at Inclusion Britain in a bit more detail. It criticises the 'lazy consensus' that racism is rife whilst simultaneously acknowledging that racism is rife. Its authors, however, take the view that their guiding mission of 'levelling up' everybody who is failing to achieve their potential will equally lift people from ethnic minorities (their preferred name for BAME people). That, in itself, fails to recognise that institutional racism creates an additional barrier to those from poor, deprived communities.

The Government response recycles some initiatives currently being tried, such as subjecting a police force's use of stop and search to more independent scrutiny – something which hadn't yet reduced the disproportionate use of it – and using more out-of-court disposal for drug, related offending.

New initiatives include guidance for employers on implementing positive discrimination in the workplace, which sounds good unless the guidance makes it more difficult to implement positive discrimination in the workplace. We shall wait and see.

The proposal to develop a 'model curriculum' which teaches children their place in a global world and the 'intertwined nature of British and Global history' by 2024 appears to be a reaction to one of the Sewell Report's biggest mistakes: the belief that there was a new story to be told about slavery, which was not about 'profit or suffering'.

It was so badly received that Sewell had to add a post-publication amendment saying they didn't mean what they wrote. There have long been calls for the school curriculum to say more about black history and maybe, just maybe, the Government have listened. The fact that any 'model curriculum' will not be mandatory, however, suggests otherwise.

Having worked in Government for decades I can imagine the number of civil servants working to produce this response with hands tied behind their backs. 'Do not say the Government disagrees, but do say the Government has listened'; 'find anything we're doing that might suggest action rather than words, stick it in and pretend it's new'; 'if you develop something interesting, say it's only "guidance" or "voluntary".'

'People only remember the headlines' is a cynical Government communication view. Then, of course, put it in the same filing cabinet in Whitehall that the other 10 reviews with a thousand recommendations currently occupies.

Meanwhile, in the same Whitehall, the Foreign, Commonwealth and Development Office were being found, by an employment tribunal, to have racially discriminated against a black senior civil servant of 33 years' service. It was, of course 'unconscious' bias that led to Sonia Warner being subjected to a six-month inquiry by her managers where the tribunal noted, 'she was treated with an unwarranted degree of suspicion, that unfair assumptions were made about her, that minds were closed, and that she was treated unfairly in the disciplinary process, which took an unreasonably long time'.

If racists run the processes then it's systemic, regardless of what the Commission's report would have you believe.

I heard multiple examples of people who were subject to extraordinary processes that frequently managed to put an incredibly positive spin on what was blatant and unsubtle racism.

Professor Binna Kandola is extremely well versed in diversity issues in senior management, having written several books on the subject. I sought his advice and we talked about bias in processes created by humans. 'There are systems that are justified by allowing some of us to get through because this is system justification theory and in slang it is tokenism,' he explained. 'I see a lack of responsibility at senior levels for this issue. For example, the colour brave policy at multi-national professional services company PricewaterhouseCoopers is not brave at all. If you expose yourself, you put yourself in danger when in fact any diversity policy if it's going to really succeed needs to be about being safe.'

He argued that it was a mistake to view racism as being a problem of the past, and it will continue to be a stain on society because of people running processes. 'Racism exists in human beings and therefore will exist in their institutions. It's not a case of "a few bad apples" because you can't have racism without racists.'

In recent years there has been significant growth in racism towards British Chinese people because of the pandemic. Kandola puts this down largely to envy, where people ask 'How is it that they get all the good jobs?' Increasingly he sees this in black and Asian dynamics, where black people have an increase in participation and representation at the expense of Asian people. This I have seen a lot of.

He adds that the challenge of identifying twenty first-century racism requires continual scrutiny of efforts to pay lip service to inclusion. 'The racist architecture means that the cladding around the building may look fair and equal but the scaffolding underneath is toxic.'

It's only fair that such scrutiny should be afforded to those who are meant to 'police' race equality, most notably the EHRC. This is an organisation whose origins were entirely in race relations, but have since expanded their remit to cover all protected characteristics with Equality legislation.

Late in 2021, an employee wrote an email to her colleagues on departing the organisation, which said that it was proving difficult to talk about race in the EHRC. The now former employee said, 'Some of our senior leadership in England has helped dismantle the backbone of the Commission, its integrity and authenticity when it comes to race. Not only am I experiencing structural and institutional racism, I now have to fight it when the EHRC tells me it doesn't exist.' The EHRC disputes that.

Two former commissioners of the EHRC publicly claimed that the decision not to reappoint them was because they had been 'too loud and vocal' about issues of race. Lord Simon Woolley and Baroness Meral Hussein-Ece are both stalwarts of the anti-racism movement and have been recognised by successive Governments for their work.

As a regulator, the EHRC has statutory powers to enforce where breaches of equality are identified. It was previously the Commission for Race Equality, and was highly regarded for some ground-breaking enforcement it had undertaken. Now it has become rolled up into a broader institution which sees race as only one of the issues it must deal with. Resources were being redirected away from race, according to both ex-commissioners, and enforcement powers were being used sparingly, if at all.

I began to think that the many examples I'd seen of fear taking hold of people and preventing them from speaking out might be more endemic than I'd imagined. We were truly in Houston: we have a problem territory when even the regulators will only speak out after they have left employment.

This became even more worrying when someone on the Media Powerlist, supposedly one of the 100 most powerful people in the industry. phoned me to admit, 'I have so much to say about this subject, but I can't put my name to it till I retire.' This conversation played out too many times with people across different industries. I could only draw one conclusion from it: it's not safe to talk about race.

The three institutions where the fear of speaking out was most palpable were the BBC, the NHS and the civil service. These are institutions which employ millions and which all of us pay for. I can't begin to tell you how many times I heard, 'If I didn't work here, I would have plenty to say.' I have, out of respect for their wishes, not named many high-profile figures who told me things that I wanted to share with you- but which would have disclosed their identities. As one put it, 'There are so many red flags, it's basically bunting'.

That's why we need an independent inquiry with the power to summon witnesses, together with the outlawing of non-disclosure agreements, which were meant to protect the identity of victims but now do nothing more than protect the institution.

Listening to Rohit Kachroo, Global News Editor at ITN, I understood how micro-aggressions cumulatively wear you down to the point that it's better not to say anything anymore. Bravely, he allows me to share some.

'It was the proudest moment of my career, picking up an award from the Royal Television Society, a few days before lockdown struck in 2020,' he explains. 'But moments after I left the stage at a swanky London hotel, I was brought back down to earth. I was wearing black tie and clutching my "Specialist Journalist of the Year" gong when an executive from a rival news broadcaster cornered me to offer congratulations – except the praise wasn't for me. "Rageh, some excellent stuff this year, well done," said this senior editor, who in their day job is tasked with making key decisions about which stories are covered and who from their newsroom gets to cover them. They had confused me with Rageh Omaar, one of Britain's best-known war reporters – my esteemed colleague who has been a household name for many years. Rageh and I don't look alike, by the way, but at least once a month another journalist will greet me using his name.

'Perhaps it's an honour to be confused with someone as widely respected as Rageh, but this is what some people refer to as "micro-aggressions". I see them less as aggressions but revelations about what's in someone's mind, how I am being perceived. For many of us, this is our role – and that awards dinner was just another reminder that while white colleagues get to be just themselves, for many of us who report on the world, who have things to say and insights to bring, our role is simply to be "the black guy", or "the brown guy" or in my case, both.'

Such instances are much more symbolic of the wider news agenda, Kachroo argues, claiming that the industry suffers from an obsession with some mythical middle England white audience.

'We overstate how much objectivity there is in the news stories we cover,' he says. 'There are so many terrible things happening in the world at any one time that we are forced to make subjective choices about what we think is important, what we care about. When we report on a case because "everyone is talking about it" or because an issue has "really cut through" (an awful phrase), we are usually thinking about a specific, hypothetical white reader, viewer or listener. When we discuss the way "real people" are reacting to a story, those real people are almost always white people.'

This mindset can at times make it harder for newsrooms to empathise with certain groups, and can make for a restrictive news agenda.

'People get confused about what racism is and isn't in newsrooms,' he admits. 'I have worked with and against very few journalists – perhaps none – who think people of one race are superior, more knowledgeable or talented, than people of another. The reality is far more nuanced. It is an inability to see that our perspective might be shaped by our circumstances, that there is no perfectly objective insight into what matters and what doesn't matter.

'Like most people from minority groups, I was forced to learn that not everyone thinks and does what I did in the school playground. I realised that most of the other kids didn't spend their Sundays eating rice and peas for dinner and writing letters to grandparents in India – so on Monday mornings I knew to adapt the way I spoke about my weekend activities if I wanted the other kids in Year Four to understand. As an adult I am forever struck by how obvious it is that so many journalists have never had to do this. It means that stories about "people like us" dominate the news, whereas atrocities abroad and scandals at home do now reach the surface. It is part of why the news agenda in the UK has become increasingly focused on Britain – well, England – even though major international stories such as the fall of Kabul to the Taliban attract huge audiences.'

White middle-aged men dominate the ranks of Britain's news media and journalism generally. An even narrower group of white men who drink in the same pubs dominate the Westminster lobby system. This shapes the way we see politics and how we see the world. It explains why research suggests that minority ethnic audiences warm to the news programmes which are perceived to best challenge 'the system' and which have the most international perspective.

In years gone by, a middle-aged white male bias didn't attract much scrutiny. But in a modern Britain held together by a rich ethnic tapestry, it feels shrunken and outdated. Clinging to this smaller, bygone Britain is no longer an option, and change is happening everywhere, albeit at varying speeds. How is the need to embrace more diversity being played out in the media? I ask.

'I have sensed a fightback in newsrooms,' says Kachroo. 'Many white journalists feel they are being punished for their skin colour. The frequency with which people share this analysis with me is revealing – it tells me that people cannot see that many of their black and Asian colleagues feel they have been paying a daily tax on their skin for their entire careers.'

One obvious grievance is that many can now only see increased opportunities for racial minority journalists – but Kachroo says this is not how it might look.

'I can see the foundations for their thinking,' he admits. 'I was 23 years old when I was allowed to file my first report for national television news. It was September 2005, the night of ITV's fiftieth birthday. I was a local reporter who had been dragged down to the national newsroom for a few weeks. I was way too young to be doing any of this and I was well aware of that. But the bosses in

London had chosen me, a rookie in a regional newsroom in Birmingham, because they needed someone from an ethnic minority to cover a story about racial silos. I was embarrassed to be reporting on the issue and determined not to be defined by the colour of my skin. I had hoped that my colleagues back in the local ITV newsroom in the Midlands would have been too drunk at the corporate birthday bash to have seen my report. When I returned to the Midlands, one colleague's first comment was "Well they obviously needed a black guy." He was right. I thought of that moment years later at the awards dinner when I was confused for Rageh Omaar.'

Kachroo's eloquent reflections ultimately left me very sad. I have watched him reporting from war zones including Ukraine and admired his every word, but I now know that, out of shot, he is often contemplating leaving the profession. Why should he? Why should anybody?

Another figure I have nothing but admiration for is Krish Majumdar, the first non-white Chair of BAFTA, the Film and Television body. What happened to him has left a gigantic 'Harry Potter-like scar' on his head.

'I was accused recently of covering up the Noel Clarke story where allegations of sexual abuse were made against the actor,' he explains when we met. 'I ended up suing *The Times* newspaper, who admitted that they had got it wrong but refused to accept that racism might have been the source of their allegation against me.'

Noel Clarke is a critically acclaimed actor screenwriter and director of colour who became the subject of numerous allegations of sexually inappropriate behaviour by several women. Clarke has 'vehemently' denied sexual misconduct and has not faced criminal prosecution. But the exposure given to these allegations was, not surprisingly, a recognition that the #MeToo movement still had work to do in highlighting a culture where sexual abuse by powerful people had allegedly been carried out on an industrial scale.

But, in looking at the Clarke allegations, Majumdar became a target for journalists. Why, might you ask? Outside of BAFTA, he has never met or worked with Clarke. They were never friends or business associates. BAFTA had given Clarke an award, but they give hundreds of awards every year and the evidence of allegations that Clarke faced were not known to the BAFTA committee that made the award. Still, it was Majumdar that they focused on.

It came as a total shock and knocked him for six. 'I'm pretty sure that I had a mental breakdown as a result of what has been thrown at me in recent years,' he tells me, 'and certainly in recent months. The campaign against me felt like a lynching. I didn't know Clarke outside of BAFTA or ever work with him. But that did not stop them from attacking me as if somehow people of colour are going to stick together.'

I've spoken before about how two black or brown people in the same building or even the same institution are often accused of being 'up to something' and are actively engaged in some conspiracy or other.

The Times newspaper apologised after a threat of legal action, publishing an article to the effect that they accepted the links they had suggested between Clarke and Majumdar were completely false. The Mail likewise apologised in similar terms. 'The stench sticks though,' reflects Majumdar. However, he is less concerned about the personal injuries he has sustained and more focused on what the industry must do to protect others.

'What I want is a level playing field,' he argues. 'This cannot be achieved while all the gatekeepers are white. You have to be on the inside, you have to have allies and you have to ensure that the commissioning is carried out by people who understand the diverse nature of this country. Quotas operate even if they don't strictly exist. I don't like the idea of just having a day where you are demonstrating how diverse you are as Channel 4 did recently with their Black to Front project. It has to be every day.'

Listening to him passionately arguing his case, I felt his pain. But I also felt his determination to rise above it and improve the conditions for everyone. The stench is hard to remove, though.

Institutions who haven't seriously addressed racism will always embarrass, denigrate and unfairly treat people of colour, whatever their publicly articulated good intentions might be.

The Sewell Commission failed to understand that or deliberately decided to ignore it.

When I moved to Manchester to take up my role as Chief Prosecutor more than a decade ago, I knew only one person in the city. Nighat Awan, OBE was a strong successful business woman who, with her husband Rafique, ran a mainly commercial property enterprise with a number of restaurants as a side project, which started more than three decades ago. Their Shere Khan restaurants were seen as a pioneer of the Manchester curry scene. In fact, the world famous 'Curry Mile' was virtually started by them. I first met her when she was invited by the Blair Government to deliver leadership training (for free) to civil service leaders. She was a friend of Cherie Blair I subsequently learnt. Nighat was heading in only one direction, up to the top, wherever that was. That is, until the police targeted her and her husband's restaurant business arm.

In 2007, a very public set of raids were undertaken at their restaurants, without warning or evidence – though the last bit wasn't known for a while. The operation was to find workers in their restaurants who may have inadequate immigration status. They had dozens of staff, mainly of south Asian heritage, as one would expect of Indian restaurants. Now, you would think that a few identity checks would ensure the matter was quickly resolved in a matter of days or weeks. This wasn't to be. Several *years* later, both Nighat and her husband were released from investigation with no evidence of immigration fraud ever being uncovered.

Meanwhile, their businesses suffered due to this sword of Damocles hanging over them. Their names were sullied in the media and the impact on their mental health was long lasting. They never found out why, they of all people, were subjected to this ordeal. But they do know that racism played its part. 'On so many occasions the officers told us that it would take as long as they wanted it to take and that given how successful we were, we must be up to something,' Nighat told me.

Now where have I heard that before? Well, pretty much everywhere.

'We never got an apology, we never knew why they chose us, but they treated us with contempt,' she recalls.

I saw first hand how their health deteriorated, their business suffered and her future career was badly damaged. But I couldn't do a thing to help her because if I even so much as asked the police for an update, I know that I too would have been dragged into the non-existent conspiracy.

As painful as it was to see decent people being unfairly pilloried, it was something I'd almost come to expect. Time and again, good people of colour have suffered at the hands of an institutional racism that we are told doesn't exist.

But it does exist and it cloys your senses. We aren't talking contrails or gossamer traces. Racism was 'in your face' and shameless. And for those on the receiving end, it wasn't a brush-by experience. You felt branded.

Almost a quarter of the way into the twenty-first century, I despair that we're still talking about racism. And I despair that we're continuing to make the same mistakes of history and are still running from the truth. They say denial is the way we handle what we can't handle and that's why everything continues to run through the filters and compressors of tunnel vision. It's the only way to provide the answers society expects – and it's the only way to keep obscuring the truth.

But as long as we continue this sick game of denial, nothing will ever be healed.

13

HOPE

Another country

I've only ever flown first class once and that was when the US Government paid for me to deliver training in New York a few years ago. When I arrived to check in wearing T-shirt and jeans, the white guy in front of me said, 'It's first class you know.' When I went to the gate after the flight was called, the white check-in lady said, 'This is first class only' and when I got on the plane and was putting my hand luggage overhead, the white guy nearby said, 'Only first class can put their bags in there.'

That is micro-aggression. Things said and done to make me feel unwanted, uncomfortable and motivated by racial bias. I'm never flying 'first class' again to be treated as second class.

Compare and contrast with the time I was invited to the launch of then Prime Minister David Cameron's well-being index in 2010. There I am minding my own business sitting at the back of a room among a couple of hundred white public sector leaders when I get a tap on my shoulder. 'I'm the PM's special adviser, would you come with me please?' You don't say no to invitations like that and so I followed her as she led me to the front, barely metres away from the lectern where Cameron was due to speak. 'Please sit there,' I was told. A few moments later Cameron came on stage and delivered his address about how the Government wants to ensure that equality is more than a buzzword.

Meanwhile photographers took numerous pictures with me looking admiringly up at him. Well I had no choice. Of course, the end result, which the PM's advisers had in mind all along, was that the media and the public get to think that the room is more diverse than it is. They needed me to create this illusion and, like a fool, I allowed them.

But all that is in the past, I told myself. The dial is starting to turn, isn't it? Then I picked a day. Any day, but let's say 16 March 2022 when I am writing this chapter.

On any particular day, there are too many cases where racism rears its ugly head. And this particular Wednesday was no different. As I poured the first coffee of the day and scanned the news head-lines, my eyes alighted on a report of an independent safeguarding review published about an incident at a school in Hackney, London.

The case involved a 15-year-old girl who was removed from an exam at school after teachers had called the police, claiming they had smelt cannabis on her (there wasn't any). Two Metropolitan Police officers subsequently took her into a room and subjected her to a degrading strip search. Not only were her intimate body parts exposed, but she was made to remove her tampon, told to bend over and spread her buttocks using her hands while coughing. No drugs were found.

This humiliating experience was authorised by her school and her parents were not told. By law, an appropriate adult should have been present, but there wasn't one. I didn't need to know her colour because I correctly guessed straight away it was black.

I know that black people are nine times more likely to be stopped and searched. The police issued an apology, but, typically, there has been no accountability. Not surprisingly, it was also acknowledged in the Safeguarding Review that racism was likely to have been an 'influencing factor' in the officers' actions. This wholly disproportionate decision to strip search the girl left her traumatised, the community aghast and public confidence in our police and institutions further damaged.

The second headline I noted that day was based on a report by the Royal Society of Chemistry (RSC), which found that of the 575 chemistry professors in the UK, only one was black.

This was Robert Mokaya, the Professor of Materials Chemistry and Pro-Vice Chancellor for Global Engagement at the University of Nottingham. The story went on to tell us that in 15 years, not one application he had submitted for research funding to the Government quango, UK Research and Innovation, had been accepted. 'That was unusual for a professor,' he helpfully added. The RSC admitted that 'racism is pervasive in the field' and this is 'hard to challenge'. It added that the marginalisation of minorities has become 'normalised' in universities and industries and that there is little incentive for chemistry organisations to improve.

Finally, my eyes moved to another page and found one of our largest trade unions, the Public and Commercial Services Union, had decided to withdraw from a UK Government Review into racism and bullying in the Cabinet Office. They accused the review of being a 'whitewash'. In their view, the 'Respect and Inclusion' review was nothing more than a 'paper exercise'.

By the time I'd read these three stories I hadn't even finished my coffee. I didn't turn the page, check the sports or do the crossword. How could I? It's all too easy to be disheartened when it's staring you in the face and happening right at the top.

And in many ways that has been the challenge of this book. I never wanted it to read like misery lit, though I have to admit there were many days when I had listened to depressing accounts when I too questioned whether there was anything to fuel optimism.

But hope is a strange thing. It tells us to cling on even when the branch is breaking. Perhaps it's because deep down we know it's all we have. But, for me, it came from my own children, from a generation often spoken of in derogatory terms for their lack of resilience, but who convinced me that they could deal with what's coming. 'Eyes wide open,' said one; 'Not going to take it,' said another.

I then decided that when I spoke to contributors, I would ask them to share something hopeful before we terminated our conversation. It has to be said, many couldn't bring themselves to do it, but others welcomed the opportunity.

BBC broadcaster Ankur Desai shared many incidents of micro-aggression, which clearly caused great pain. But, he told me, 'The lesson I learned, was that there are going to be hurdles which are often too high to jump over for one reason or another, but that would not diminish my work ethic and desire to achieve my dreams in this industry. I promised myself that I would surpass anything that role may have offered me at the time, and I would like to think I have achieved that. There are structural obstacles which have existed for years. But, I feel I am part of a generation who are smashing through them in double-quick time, and the next generation are taking up the baton with even more gusto.'

Professor Tahir Abbas left the country for mainland Europe after a series of attacks, but he remained optimistic. 'While racism is pervasive, there will always be prominent and influential white people who make things happen for us people of colour, so it's not the case that every single white apple is a rotten one,' he told me. 'But it only takes one or two for the entire system to go bad. What I must say is that people under the age of 30, as well as my students in their early twenties, are often far more concerned with race, equality and diversity than they were 20 or 30 years ago.'

As the third black woman ever to be elected as an MP, Dawn Butler made history by becoming the first ever elected female African Caribbean minister to speak at the Dispatch Box, as well as the first ever MP to use British Sign Language to ask a question in the House of Commons. She described truly terrible racially motivated attacks on her and her staff, including some that led to convictions, but declared, 'So, everything is a battle, every step of the way. But it is not just about the battles but the war. I think if we all work together, call it out and don't stand for it, then we can win the war on racism and discrimination.'

All the signs of hope that I heard were also wrapped up in courage. Dawn was not the only one who saw the future in terms of 'fights', 'battles' and 'wars'.

Unzela Khan relayed many racially motivated battles in her journalism career, which has taken her to senior editorial roles at a relatively young age. But she was still quick to encourage those starting out. 'What I will say to the next generation . . . is to fight your corner. Every single time I have faced small or big challenges when it comes to race, I have made sure to let people know that this is not acceptable. There are very few journalists from ethnic minority backgrounds, and the reason for this is that we stop at the first hurdle when we feel like we don't belong. But that's why we need to make sure we show them we are here to stay.'

I've known and respected Zahed Amanullah, Resident Senior Fellow at ISD Global, for a few years given his work in understanding radicalisation. When he related the racism he saw taking root in towns across Britain, I was struck by the community support he identified in one town that had fallen victim to race riots 20 years ago.

'When the EDL [English Defence League] gathered at the entrance of a cul-de-sac for a march in Bradford near a relative's house where I was staying, the white neighbours gathered at the entrance in case the marchers spotted the lone Asian family,' he explained. 'They were protective following years of neighbourliness on both sides.'

What Ellisha Soanes doesn't know about being a black educator isn't worth knowing. So it was delightful to hear her offer this insight: 'I helped to steer the first college in the UK to teach black history all year round, moving away from the dedicated one month per year we all know. I did this by talking to my own students and hearing their experiences, which were similar to my own.

'Purposefully, my students and I decided not to elaborate on civil rights or slavery. As imperative as these elements are to our history, these make up a small segment of black history. I wanted to create more awareness on areas that are rarely discussed in the education sector, such as ancient Kemet, African royalty, inventors, the Windrush generation and so much more, to inspire the next generation especially from diverse backgrounds.'

It's this kind of positivity that begins to kindle the first sparks of hope, at least for the next generation.

I heard this from Anjula Singh, erstwhile Director of Communication at the Labour Party: 'I continue to dream about public service institutions being braver and actually removing structural barriers, generational privilege and people who are block-ers instead of overlaying bad systems with diversity schemes and targets. The alternative would be to give up, and that I refuse to do – as a child of immigrants I am driven to build on the sacrifices they made for my generation.'

I recognise that drive, the belief that our parents suffered more than we did and that we owe it to them.

Strength in numbers certainly helped Ashish Joshi, a highly experienced broadcaster currently at Sky News. 'The more representation we have then we are less likely to feel isolated and exposed,' he explains. 'We have a very strong network of Sky staff from minority backgrounds on a WhatsApp forum. We feel free to share ideas, thoughts and raise concerns. Less senior colleagues can ask for help and guidance in navigating what can be a daunting workscape. I did not have the benefit of anything like this when I first started in media. It's good to know there are people who have undergone the same journey and are there to steer you if you need.'

It's evident that the burden of addressing racism falls disproportionately on those who are victims of it. You wouldn't expect rape
victims to tackle the male violence driven by misogyny that causes
them to be a victim. No one would seriously suggest putting the
responsibility on those who suffer and yet we don't think twice
about expecting people of colour to lead our work on anti-racism,
to be our EDI managers, and to be the ones that try to change the
status quo.

Gloria Hyatt was the first black headteacher in Liverpool and
this is what she told me.

'I educated myself on racism so I could confidently educate
others, young and old, and I wrote this into curriculums when
teaching. I mentored black children so they could believe and
achieve, I role modelled it in my behaviours, so it was more than
just words. I employed a diverse teaching staff and elevated black
Asian and minority people to leadership positions. I sat on boards
and in positions of influence and spoke the language of these peers
so they got to experience an educated black person and achieve
learning that they could take back into their classrooms, their
workplaces, their communities, their families.'

She was obliged to fix things because she could, and used her
experiences of racism to ensure, as best she could, that others didn't
face the same obstacles. Could the same be said about the white
headteachers?

Yasmin Somani has had several roles in public sector leadership
and has been called a friend of 'suicide bombers' to her face, but
her optimism (and it's not misplaced) continually shines through.

'I sincerely believe society has the capability and appetite to
largely overcome prejudice and racism, and in my opinion there are
several parts to this,' she explains. 'Firstly, members of ethnic
minorities must not be dissuaded from taking up roles in society,
from furthering their positions, to be seen, heard and contribute to
a society which is diverse and a true reflection of the melting pot

that Britain is today. Secondly – of course I am not the first to say it and I will not be the last – it is education. The root of racism is fear which is cultivated by a lack of education and knowledge. Society must shift its position from fearing the unknown to understanding it, through schools, through workplaces and ultimately through the media who must be held accountable for the narrative they often irresponsibly perpetuate. I also believe real change will depend on the essential role ethnic groups themselves have to play; communities should be open and contribute to the learning process and communities should be empowered to do so. The true realisation of a well-rounded and functioning society in relation to race will be a complex one, with many layers, and it will require time and consistency. In order for us to achieve this, the dialogue regarding race from all parties should be an open one, without too much concern about not using the right words or being politically correct – sometimes people need to ask the difficult questions to educate themselves and if parts of society are too apprehensive to speak up in the fear that there will be a backlash then we aren't truly having the conversations and growing the knowledge which we need. To genuinely make a change for future generations we need to build trust, openness and integrations across communities and truly embed these bonds within society. It is then that we'll all start to see humanity and not the colour of each other's skin.'

There were other signs too that suggested change was stirring in the national psyche. In all walks of life, an encouraging narrative is forming, which suggests our major institutions will have to do things differently. And the message of diversity is not just coming from the usual suspects. See the argument made by the former commander of a nuclear submarine, Vice Admiral Nick Hine, that our armed forces need to recruit more neurodiverse people, for example. The military, he insisted, had to recruit from a much wider pool if Britain wished to compete with other nations that had larger defence budgets.

'If you want to transform, if you want a different way of doing business, you can't keep asking the same question of the same people and expect a different answer,' he argued.

I couldn't have put it better myself.

You can also see it in the work of tech entrepreneurs like Khyati Sundaram. After sending hundreds of CVs out to try and get a job and barely receiving a response, she realised there were too many biases at play in recruitment systems. So she decided to put her AI and coding skills to good effect and developed a behavioural science tool for predictive and fair hiring.

As she told *The Times*, her software is 'built on the premise that we will give you the information that is right and good to help you make that hiring decision and take away what is irrelevant and noise, for instance what my name sounds like, where I went to school.'

Her platform has already been used by companies such as Pepsi to asses half a million applications and has increased ethnic minority roles in technology by 50 per cent.

And I see it in the dawning recognition in the business community that UK plc will continue to struggle with skills shortage problems unless it embraces diversity.

'We are struggling to recruit from a truly diverse talent pool,' admits the Advertising Association President Alessandra Bellini. 'It is vital we make our industry one where everyone feels they belong.' Even the Confederation of British Industry is encouraging ethnicity pay reporting and demanding that we become a country known for diversity and inclusion where 'everyone can bring their authentic self to work, irrespective of background, age, gender, sexuality, race or disability.'

And it's also there in the ground-breaking employment tribunal battles to expose racism and hold bad businesses to account. For example, women like Semhar Tesfagiorgis, who successfully sued an exclusive London casino after they prevented her from working at the table of a patron who requested 'females with fair skin'.

Good people will always inspire hope and the deeds of individuals are often what start the process of change. There are many sparks lighting a fire. But a decisive shift also requires systems to make sure change reaches everybody. And I wasn't so sure I felt sufficiently hopeful that the right foundations were yet in place.

The gatekeepers for senior leadership include the HR departments and the recruitment agents. Absurdly, comically and ironically there is poor diversity in the roles responsible for recruitment of talent and ensuring equity and inclusion. The Green Park Business Leaders Index 2021 research, published in August 2021, shows that HR is dominated by white women, at 55 per cent. And ethnic minority women in leadership positions of Diversity and Inclusion are at 22.9 per cent, while ethnic minority males are the least represented at 6.3 per cent.

Old explanations of 'couldn't find qualified personnel' are no longer possible to justify. Yet it is evident from recent data that the people who are supposed to be pushing diversity and enforcing inclusion are themselves not representative of minority groups.

The Green Park Index did show some more promising results – an additional 107 ethnic minority Board and Executive Committee leaders over the last eight years, which is an upward climb to 10.4 per cent. The prognosis for this level is not as grim as for Chairs, Chief Executives and Chief Financial Officers. At this rate, the FTSE 100 is three to four years away from being proportionately representative of the UK population at this level. That said, the main growth is in Chief Financial Officer roles – cue lots of comments about ethnic minorities being good at accounting.

Whenever I feel that hope is in short supply, I ask my children. All are in their early twenties and they are all following their passions.

Marina, my eldest, is following the legal path despite my various attempts to stop her.

'I studied in Bristol where I was proud to see the Colston statue brought down with a rise of residents speaking out to remove slave trader references from numerous places around the city. As I progress in my career, I am motivated to be part of the process of removing inequality from the justice system and in particular prison reform and police reform. I want to see more accountability from the police and more checks to decisions that they make. If I can achieve some change, then I will be happy with my stamp on this Earth.'

Shaan, my eldest son, is a graduate of Glasgow University and is pursuing a career in policy think tanks.

'The reason that I am optimistic arises from the fact that I know that – no matter how terrible things still are – racism overall is weaker than when my parents were in the same position that I am. My hope for the future is to have a decent paying job working somewhere that I can influence policy such as through a think tank or similar organisation. I believe that "purpose" is found through serving others, and hope to do this in my day-to-day to leave a better legacy for my future children.'

Samir is about to graduate in music production and has the self-taught ability to play several instruments, particularly guitar.

'I'm fortunate that unlike many other professions, the music industry has always had a progressive lead compared to other aspects of society, as through art we all become equal and are able to share experiences.

'Unlike many other minorities, I am lucky that I have a father who has worked so hard to put me and my siblings in a situation of privilege where many of the barriers that already exist will not be as hard to break down. It is vital that we aim to equalise this and give many opportunities to disadvantaged minorities, providing them with the skills and access points to break through unnecessary discrimination. But I am hopeful that social progress will not slow. What I consider important, however, is that we do not alienate people in society with how we go about bringing this change. If we want a positive change, we must allow people to learn to become better.'

Last but not least is my youngest, Kabir, who has a creative talent for writing 'beats' which others seem to really love.

'My dream has always been to be a music producer – specifically in the world of hip-hop. This is a genre often slandered in the media, but the reality tells a different story, when one realises how diverse and beautiful it can be. You've got people from all backgrounds, of any age, gender or race, not just doing very well for themselves, but doing it based on their own merit. The genre was built off rebellion against those in power – from Public Enemy to Dave in our time – and thrives off allowing people to be what they want to be, not what they are told to be.'

Allowing people to be what they want to be and letting everyone fulfil their potential is a sentiment that's almost childlike in its simplicity. It's an ideal we can all get behind. And yet it's become maddeningly difficult and impossibly complex.

When you look at Britain today, it may consist of four nations. But it's divided between two worlds. The first is Britain of the past, which is still anchored in John Major's vision of a country of long shadows on county grounds, warm beer, invincible green suburbs, dog lovers and pools fillers and, as George Orwell said, 'Old maids bicycling to holy communion through the morning mist'. This is a country that's rural and white and attuned to the sounds of church bells, gentle applause and the smack of leather on willow. It's the green and fair land of Hardy, Tennyson and Kipling. The country of Elgar and Vaughan Williams.

But there is another country that's altogether more urban, diverse and modern. It's a nation of tower blocks, Glastonbury and curry. A stylish and creative, tech-fuelled powerhouse. An outward facing multi-lingual Britain that's streaming, dreaming and meme-ing. Soundtracked by ringtones, the grinding of espresso machines and tram horns. A republic of fierce music, sassy start-ups, change-makers and cultural giants.

This is a country that understands and respects Britain's past without wishing to permanently camp there. It's one that sees the roadblocks in our path but refuses to change course, guided by the belief that Britain does not have to remain pickled in aspic and can be shaped as it should be; fairer, better and bigger. It's a land where a sassy, smart and confident next generation wants more than their parents had – and demands a new social contract for our times.

Every day you will see glimpses of this country. It sashays across our cultural airwaves and disrupts our rituals. Like a restless, impatient future, it hovers above, biding its time until the stars will eventually swing into place. Sooner or later the moment will arrive when this future calls time on an outdated past and turns the switch.

I see it all the time. But, for the most part, as a country, we only see flashes of this future, brimming with purpose in the work of pioneering music entrepreneurs like Jamal Edwards, who sadly died too young. Or in Wayne Jordash QC, who fought his way to the top to become one of the most internationally renowned human rights lawyers. With a working-class, mixed-heritage background, he had, not surprisingly, thought that becoming a QC was not for 'people like me', but refused to lower his sights. Working in a newsagents in Peckham, a bookmakers and a factory while he studied law, his results were originally withheld as he did not have the money to pay the Bar School fees.

But, while the obstacles remain high and the roadblocks too numerous, talent sometimes finds a way. Jordash was awarded a QC in 2014 and says he was surprised at how the QC Panel were willing to 'look outside the norm – or, rather, at what was generally perceived as the norm'. We need to see more of this perspective coming to panels, boards and selection committees everywhere.

Many still see this Britain as a threat and they shouldn't. It seeks to enrich, not tear down our collective history and rich traditions. It should be viewed as a bridge between Britain's past and future and a means to fully unlock our potential.

There is another country in these isles that has been ignored for too long. And its time has come to shine.

CONCLUSION

When I sat down to write this, I expected to be drafting a list of recommendations to help transform our country and make it easier for talented people of colour to rise to the top.

In the course of many conversations, meetings and late night emails, I saw countless areas where casual discrimination was rife. At its worst, this was exclusion funded by the taxpayer. Sport was one of the most egregious examples and it's hard to see how the Government can continue to fund countless sporting bodies that allow discrimination to flourish on their watch.

At a time when public health is deteriorating in many communities across the UK, how can it be that numerous sporting bodies continue to hoover up public funding while making no effort to widen participation rates in their sport? Why is the taxpayer continuing to fund virtual sporting apartheid in golf, cycling, tennis and rowing clubs in Britain?

But, as I began to compile a list of recommendations, one thought suddenly stopped me. My mind turned to my conversation with the Archbishop of Canterbury in which he'd complained that hundreds of recommendations in church reports had yet to be delivered. How many other reports like this, filled with important recommendations that could make a huge difference, are gathering dust in filing cabinets, I wondered?

There are probably hundreds, if not thousands, and that's why there's no point making recommendations until they're able to land in an environment where they will be taken seriously and acted upon.

But how, then, do you create that environment where a commitment to serious change will be made?

It ultimately starts at the top.

And it begins with a change in our political discourse, which sets the tone for everything.

For too long now there's been a lazy consensus among the political classes around the idea of Britain being a meritocracy. It hasn't been for a long time, if it ever was, and keeping this dead idea on a life support machine only detracts from the real issue our politicians should be examining: that much of Britain is run by a rigged system.

This is not even cleverly concealed anymore. It's there for all to see, and grotesquely parades itself in large parts of public life, from the civil service to the police, where ethnic minority leaders continue to remain conspicuously absent. Year on year it manifests itself in numerous individual stories, ranging from Professor Robert Mokaya's 15 years of being refused research funding to Azeem Rafiq's painful exposure of inhuman racist abuse.

It's a system that's tainted by prejudice and continues to rely on nepotism, cronyism and a tiny pool of Oxbridge talent to determine who runs our institutions and organisations. And it's a system that continues to degrade and diminish what's long been seen as a core value of the UK: fairness.

While politicians ostensibly cling to the idea of meritocracy and opportunities in life being dependent on how hard you work, their actions show they don't believe this at all. Parliament is awash with cronyism and chumocracy. Politicians don't even pretend to hide it anymore. Failed ministers with close links to Prime Ministers are rewarded with bigger and better jobs; multi-million pound contracts are handed over to friends and party political associates; and even nominations to the House of Lords are determined by who you know rather than your potential contribution to public life.

There are unedifying examples of this latter instance everywhere. But the process of selecting the Conservative candidate for Dover and Deal a few years ago takes some beating. In this safe Tory seat, the MP, Charlie Elphicke, was jailed after being convicted of sexual assault. But rather than commit to a fresh start and bring in a new broom to scrub away Elphicke's stench, his wife Natalie inherited the seat without an open selection process. It was described as a grubby deal to keep the seat warm for her husband, but was yet another hammer blow to democracy.

How any politician can possibly balance actions like this, and the brazen desire to preserve inherited privilege, corporate welfare and cronyism with a desperate pretence that Britain is a great meritocracy where hard work is rewarded, is increasingly untenable.

It's a balancing act that's becoming harder to pull off. And the public are starting to notice. Witness the backlash that former *Love Island* contestant and 'influencer' Molly-Mae Hague received when she claimed in an interview that 'if you want something enough, you can achieve it' regardless of income or social background. Among the barrage of criticism that poured her way were frequent comments that social inequality meant there would never be a level playing field.

Yet still the idea that an individual's success is determined by talent and effort alone remains deeply entrenched and it will take a brave politician to challenge this.

But challenge it they must. For unless our political leaders face up to the fact that Britain is losing a war on talent, with vast potential going to waste every day, then we will become smaller, poorer and more isolated.

This conversation must start somewhere and perhaps it will begin when a politician stands before a podium and doesn't have an audience containing handpicked black and brown faces before them to keep up this pretence.

Maybe then they could start to speak honestly about the meritocracy myth and address the people who aren't in the room and are probably no longer even listening. This is what we must do to face up to the fact that Britain is no longer sharing opportunity with those who work the hardest. And the reason for this is because our institutions have become corrupted by cronyism, nepotism and inherited privilege.

If just a tiny fraction of this truth entered our public discourse, it would start to shake up our monolithic political culture and begin the necessary work of reversing years of reactionary rhetoric.

Instead of having to endure politicians framing Britain's challenges as a battle between strivers and shirkers, it's time we talked about failed leaders and the failure to realise Britain's potential. No more should we hear politicians using language to set neighbour against neighbour, such as George Osborne's infamous speech in which he questioned the fairness of a shift worker going to work, looking up at 'the closed blinds of their next door neighbour sleeping off a life on benefits'.

Instead we need to hear our leaders asking where is the fairness in comparing inherited privilege and mediocrity with real talent and hard work? Or the fairness of the hardworking and exceptionally talented Brits continually losing out on promotions to nepotism and prejudice. What has happened to our country? When did this blessed plot cease to be a hothouse for talent and became a growbag for cronyism?

CONCLUSION

There are many reasons why I don't expect to hear this speech soon, but an underlying one is that too many are afraid of the culture war.

This ugly phenomenon now dominates our politics and, as much as its phoniness frequently depresses me, it's a battle over modern values that must be won.

I've never believed in pitting one group against another, and at the heart of this book is a wish not to grow resentment but to see all communities working together more productively to ensure opportunity is equally shared.

This won't happen, though, unless there's an acceptance of the barriers preventing people's talents being realised.

And the first battle is to reclaim the word 'woke', which was appropriated from African American vernacular to become a political lightning rod. Its original meaning has been lost as it's now frequently used to mock the struggles of under-represented groups. It's become a catch-all term to lazily dismiss their grievances.

Adopted by Black Lives Matter activists in the 2010s, the origins of this idiom lie in early twentieth-century social activism and black American culture. From the Jamaican activist Marcus Garvey, to the American blues singer Lead Belly, who advised people 'best stay woke', it was used as a rallying call to stay alert to social injustice. Being 'woke' is the opposite of being asleep, seeing the injustice in inequality. But today it's a term regularly thrown at you if you challenge the unfair treatment of minorities.

As such, a cartoon-like and polarised narrative has been framed as a struggle between Canute-types trying to hold back a tide of social change and virtue signalling puritans. Like many other sham societal divides, it generates searing heat but zero light.

The big divide was never between Leave and Remain, or black and white, men and women, or north versus south. It's between those with power and those without. The power differential is the greatest cause of inequality. However, if you're a black woman from the north then you're likely to be the greatest victim of inequality. 'Just don't talk about it,' scream the anti-woke brigade.

At its most pernicious, anti-woke fundamentalism cruelly ascribes some sort of warped post-truth thinking to the progress or travails of people of colour in the public eye. I've heard it and seen it countless times, and not just in relation to others. On plenty of occasions it's been directed at me.

I got promoted because of 9/11.

I was awarded an OBE because it was the brown person's turn.

I was selected as Muslim prosecutor to prosecute other Muslims.

I was forced to resign as CEO of the Police Commissioner after the terror attack at the Manchester Arena.

Every one of these statements is a lie.

But each one of them was levelled at me by different white senior leaders who felt they could say it without consequence.

Every statement was meant to belittle me and my work.

And at the time, there was little I could do other than prove them wrong.

Anti-woke mania is gathering pace, though. And bogus battle lines are being drawn all the time. Culture wars are being fabricated in education, the arts, museums and heritage sectors. As awareness of current and historic injustices continues to grow and communities actively resist racism, regressive forces train their weapons ever more aggressively on them.

Ministers obsessively fire out letters warning museums not to remove statues of slave traders or demanding schools not to talk about race in the classroom. Many of these warnings are frequently laced with the threat of funding being withdrawn – and cumulatively it wears people down.

No one who speaks publicly about fairness and equality can escape the anti-woke attacks. Even Gareth Southgate, the England football manager, was on the receiving end, ironically, as he led the national football side to their most successful tournament for 55 years.

After Southgate wrote an open letter to England supporters challenging inequality in 2021, he had his card marked. 'I have never believed that we should just stick to football,' Southgate opined, before addressing the racists attacking his players and booing the national side when they took the knee before matches.

'Unfortunately for those people that engage in that kind of behaviour, I have some bad news,' he said. 'You're on the losing side. It's clear to me that we are heading for a much more tolerant and understanding society, and I know our lads will be a big part of that. I am confident that young kids of today will grow up baffled by old attitudes and ways of thinking.'

Soon after, newspapers reported that some Tory MPs were not happy about this and felt that Southgate had become 'a tool of deep woke'. One Tory MP, Lee Anderson, even said that he would no longer watch England 'whilst they are supporting a political movement whose core principles aim to undermine our very way of life', in response to players taking the knee.

Incredibly, Government ministers also defended England fans who booed the national team when they peacefully protested against discrimination, injustice and inequality.

It was an astonishing moment. To see MPs briefing the media against an England football manager and defending fans who booed the team all because they wished to raise awareness of inequality and discrimination showed how low we had sunk as a nation. When you consider how frequently the wholly unfair charge of being unpatriotic is levelled at people of colour, I found it staggering to see people in Government turning against their national football team at a time when they were inspiring millions.

These actions and the febrile environment that many in power are actively creating to push back against the progress of social movements has made Britain a major manufacturer of fear.

I've seen clear evidence of this in researching this book. The fear stopping people from speaking out is so tangible, you can almost smell it.

Nowhere is this more evident than in the public sector, where I spent half my working life. Surely, they, with their heavy unionisation, staff networks, strong HR departments and equality duties must get it, I thought? The reality is, that's where I found the greatest fear. People refusing point blank to go on the record despite sharing horrific examples of overt racism. Many had signed non-disclosure agreements, others were pursuing grievances and tribunals, and most just thought that their progression would be halted. 'Troublemakers' was the least offensive epithet used.

Supposedly powerful, very senior and often high-profile individuals told me that speaking to me on the record about what had happened to them or others around them was 'career ending' or at the very least damaging to their prospects. 'I wouldn't be able to face people around me if I told you how they make me feel,' said one.

Whistleblowers, too, will face the wrath of those they expose. Look at how they become targets, how their past lives are dissected with relish, in order to suggest that they cannot be credible – even when they still have the receipts. Time and time again, their courage is undermined by others.

If powerful people of colour can't or won't speak up, if those who should be vaccinated against repercussions decide they're not sufficiently immune, then what hope for those on the way up? I felt ashamed when some told me that they just couldn't expose the reality of their experiences.

I was hugely disappointed in some who were quick to jump on the disclosures by the brave few and say things such as, 'I think what Azeem [Rafiq] did was so important and necessary, cricket really needs to sort itself out.' But in the same breath, they would add, 'I just wish I had his courage.' Courage? His career was never allowed to reach its full potential, but yours has already put you in the list of the top 100 in your profession.

I was tempted to name them all so that a parliamentary select committee might then have the balls to summon them to give evidence, or better still instigate a judicial inquiry. But they will have to make that decision themselves. I hope they do. Until they do, the debate will be disjointed and incomplete.

What does all this tell you about Britain at this moment in time?

Government now legislates to outlaw protest and stifle dissent. Police intervene unlawfully in peaceful candlelit vigils for a woman raped and murdered by a serving police officer. Black Lives Matter is seen as a threat to national security, and taking a knee has been described as a weapon of woke.

It tells me that we have become world leaders in shutting down difficult conversations.

And, of course, that's how the defenders of inherited privilege would prefer to keep it.

This may keep a tiny percentage of the population happy, but the rest of us cannot be so insouciant if we wish to prevent Britain from becoming a fading power.

Because leadership matters. It's what guides others to success and inspires us to do more and become more. It sets standards and fosters a culture of humility and hard work. Leadership is what translates vision into action; it's the difference between mediocrity and greatness.

And right now, I'm not alone in seeing something rotten in our leadership. 'Britain needs a new era of serious leaders,' argues the *Financial Times*. Meanwhile, auditors have warned of a 'post-Covid organisational culture crisis' at UK companies. And others are fast recognising that changes at the top are needed.

'A series of company failures – whether that be BHS, Carillion, Greensill or Patisserie Valerie – have demonstrated why cultivating a healthy culture, underpinned by the right tone from the top, is fundamental to business success,' said Sir Jon Thompson, Chief Executive of the Financial Reporting Council.

Where might these new leaders come from? They 'may emerge in much more porous, less class-siloed societies than our own, where their lived experience allows them to reach out to build broad coalitions,' argues the respected commentator, Will Hutton.

Yet I don't believe we need to look abroad for great examples of future leadership. There are plenty here in our communities of colour; they just need to be given the chance.

Britain is facing a crisis of identity that we can no longer ignore. It's not just that the Union has never been more in peril. Or that these are dangerous times for the Monarchy. Our centuries-old history of multiculturalism and rich diversity has yet to fully coalesce around a common, shared identity.

This is laid bare in reports such as the 2017 Aurora Humanitarian Index survey, which showed that more than half of Britons believe their culture is threatened by ethnic minorities living in the UK. Furthermore, a quarter think immigrants take jobs away and a third think they remove more from society than they contribute.

Clearly this shows that much work needs to be done to heal Britain's fractured identity. And it's time we lifted the veil on who we really are as a country. Why are ministers continuing to force-fully prevent schools from educating people about the contributions made to Britain by people of colour? And why are our airwaves and media still seeking to deepen social divisions and sow distrust under the banner of culture wars?

Archaeological discoveries have shown that there have been black people in Britain for centuries, dating back to Roman times. It's a myth to think that the first time a black face was spotted on this sceptred isle was when they disembarked from the *Windrush* at Tilbury docks in 1948. People of colour are much more inextrica-bly wound up in Britain's history than most think.

CONCLUSION

Studies at University College London have also shown that immigrants arriving in the UK since 2000 have made consistently positive fiscal contributions regardless of their area of origin. In other words, immigrants add more to society than they take out.

There are many stubborn myths around people of colour in Britain, which have been unequivocally disproven – and yet they still persist. Our work will not be complete until they're permanently debunked.

Every person I spoke to in writing this book shared one deeply personal perspective. They all loved Britain. No matter how maddening, divisive or unjust our country has become, they did not want to be anywhere else.

They all believed a better future was worth fighting for and that victory could be achieved.

History tells us that the battle for equality, however long, frustrating and painful, does ultimately bend towards justice.

That is the same message I took from the many leaders I interviewed for this book. All were doing ground-breaking things, bearing huge responsibilities and helping redefine modern Britain. No matter how much abuse they faced, how constrained their job had become or the pressures they faced on a day-to-day basis, I found their struggle uplifting. In their leadership I saw an inspiring message that the next generation must seize and build on.

We are no longer fighting for a seat on the bus. We want a place at the top table. And we won't rest until we get it.

EPILOGUE

When you've studied something long enough, you begin to think you have a firm grasp of the subject. But sometimes the truth about racism hits you right between the eyes and knocks you sideways. It's then that you truly realise the system is broken and reform cannot wait a second longer.

It was the summer of 2022 and the kettle was humming on the top floor of offices in Victoria Street, London. My team and I were preparing for a day of interviews with firefighters as part of the Independent Cultural Review of London Fire Brigade, which I had been commissioned to chair. Coffee and tea were made, and plates of biscuits laid out, as I awaited our first appointment.

The review into workplace culture had been announced by London Fire Brigade Commissioner Andy Roe in November 2021 following the suicide of a black 21-year-old trainee firefighter Jaden Francois-Esprit.

Amid accusations of bullying and racism, Jaden had made 16 transfer requests to move from Wembley station before taking his life – and Roe had admitted that a culture of casual racism was deeply entrenched in some pockets of London Fire Brigade.

In an interview with the *Guardian* a year earlier, he had acknowledged that these cultural problems meant he wouldn't feel comfortable with his daughter working there.

'The benchmark for me is I've got a young mixed-heritage daughter. Can I say with confidence that she will be treated with dignity and respect in every single part of the London fire brigade? No I can't,' he admitted.

That year he also gave evidence to the Grenfell Inquiry and told Parliament that he had witnessed racism from colleagues after a fire involving a family from the Somali community.

He had been at London Fire Brigade since 2002 and, having been appointed Commissioner in 2020, he knew this was his chance to finally face down toxic cultures and behaviours that had been allowed to fester for too long.

I had few dealings with him during our year-long review, as he let us get on with our work independently. But at the outset he had ensured me and my team were given access to all 102 fire stations across London and told we could speak to anyone we wanted.

That had enabled us to reach out far and wide. It took a while to build trust with staff, because there was widespread fear about speaking out. But soon word got round that we were offering a genuine safe space in which they could talk freely about issues affecting them in their jobs. This had never been provided before and soon our inbox started to fill with requests for an interview.

We had managed to negotiate office space with Transport for London, as firefighters had made it clear they did not want to meet on Fire Brigade property because they were afraid they would be spotted. So when the first firefighters checked in and took the lift upstairs, I wasn't sure what to expect.

I knew how the drip, drip, drip effect of systemic racism took its toll. But I wasn't prepared to hear dedicated public servants explain, in gut-wrenching terms, how they had been stripped of their confidence, self-worth and dignity by racist bullies.

Over that day in the summer of 2022, I heard from over a dozen black firefighters and support staff.

There were no raised voices or theatrics. They described their experiences in a plaintive and matter of fact way and shared WhatsApp messages, emails and documented complaints. Some even had medical certificates showing they were suffering from PTSD.

These were all brave firefighters with a strong record of service. Some had been at Grenfell, and they were all used to running into harm's way to rescue people.

Quite a few couldn't hold back the tears as they recounted what had happened to them and very quickly, we ran out of tissues. A Muslim firefighter told us how he'd been repeatedly and aggressively taunted over his faith. His colleagues had put pork sausages in his pockets, posted terrorist hotline stickers on his locker and continually asked him if there was a bomb in his rucksack and whether he was 'going on Al-Qaeda terrorist training?'

Many others corroborated this racist culture. One female firefighter told us that it was an incredibly laddish environment with people constantly making racist and sexist jokes.

'They are always going on about "Muzzers",' she said. 'We had terrorism training and my watch kept pointing out of the window at brown people. "There's one, there's one and another" they kept saying."

A litany of racist incidents were shared with us that day, with one black firefighter telling us how his colleagues had put a noose over his locker as some kind of sick joke.

But as repulsive as these were, it wasn't the incidents themselves that sickened me the most. It was the cumulative impact of weeks, months and years of toxic abuse by the perpetrators on committed public servants.

All were affected and you could see in their eyes that running a daily gauntlet of humiliation left them bereft of confidence and stripped of their dignity. In some cases, you could see in their eyes that something deep inside was broken. I realised that it wasn't just that racism was poisoning institutions, it was eviscerating any trace of human dignity in the process.

But even so, they wouldn't leave because they were proud of the job and had an incredible sense of public duty.

'Why did you join the fire service,' I asked one Muslim firefighter, after realising he'd taken a pay cut from his previous job. 'Because I wanted to put something back into my community,' he said, wiping the tears from his face.

Every person of colour I spoke to, shared an enormous sense of pride in the job. 'Driving a fire engine around my community gets you a lot more respect than driving a BMW or Mercedes,' one told me.

Others spoke of wearing their uniforms when going shopping in their local superstore because people would come up to them and shake their hand. Everywhere they went dressed as firefighters they got respect. The horrible irony was that if they weren't wearing uniforms they would probably be followed by store detectives.

I had many more days of interviews like this and heard of so many assaults on people's dignity that I could feel the bile rising as I tried to process their experiences. I felt exhausted and repulsed, but above all I felt a huge sense of loss. I felt the fire brigade, and many other organisations, were losing out on a wealth of talent. Organisations like this should be seeking to get the best out of their people and prepare them to become future leaders, not grind their faces in the dirt.

When I came to submit my final review, Andy Roe looked mortified as I went through a catalogue of incidents with him. As someone who had been at Grenfell and was absolutely committed to public service, this was a hammer blow to him and I could see he was ashamed. I don't think he expected it to be this bad and I knew he felt just as sick as I did, as I told him I was going to say that London Fire Brigade was institutionally racist.

My reasoning was because after a year of studying the organisation and speaking to its staff, there was ample evidence showing that people of colour are more likely to fail courses, more likely to be disciplined, more likely to be asked to repeat training at training school, less likely to be promoted and less likely to hold senior positions. Similarly, they are still subject to abhorrent racist abuse of which we heard far too many accounts.

Until there is better representation of BAME employees across all areas of London Fire Brigade, particularly in positions of leadership, and until racists have no place in the Brigade, and do not feel they can act with impunity, then it cannot claim to be a modern and inclusive public service.

He swallowed hard as I told him this, but he accepted every word and every one of our 23 recommendations.

When the report was finally published it led the News at Ten bulletins and appeared on the front page of the *Sunday Times*. It would ultimately trigger multiple investigations in other fire and rescue services and bring other stories of prejudice and toxic behaviours to light in all parts of the country. The Chief Inspector of Fire and Rescue Services also demanded that every fire service notify him of all misconduct cases in England.

At the time, Roe faced extreme criticism and fronted dozens of tough TV and broadcast interviews. Never at any point did he attempt to defend or deflect from the behaviour of those whose behaviour had caused so much distress among his colleagues. Instead, he pledged to start the hard work of change straight away.

In one particularly tough interview with Channel 4 News, he was asked 'If you were a black person, would you join London Fire Brigade today after reading that report?'

It was a good question, but I was impressed by his response:

I could understand why you might choose not to but I would say to all people out there in London who might be considering joining London Fire Brigade....you are joining now at a point where you have probably never been safer because this is out in the open. We are making immediate change. We are facing the problem head on and I need you to join to be part of the change.

It was the kind of leadership that many more institutions in Britain needed to show and I saw straight away that Roe got it. He knew that a modern institution must be inclusive, and he was determined to drive out the poisonous behaviours that were holding his organisation back.

Roe had a deep passion for public service. He was a former army officer who had survived a pipe bomb being thrown at him, which killed the officer stood next to him. And he was insistent that London Fire Brigade had to serve all the communities of the capital equally.

Of course, the proof will be in how Roe turns around London Fire Brigade. But I was left in no doubt that he was deeply committed to making change happen.

Sadly, the same cannot be said for many other leaders across our country.

Rishi Sunak became our first Prime Minister of colour on October 22, 2022. I found it genuinely moving seeing him celebrate Diwali at a Downing Street reception and It should have been a moment signifying that Britain is finally an inclusive country where all races and creeds have the same opportunity to rise according to their talents. It ought to have symbolised the moment when we could finally start consigning racism to the dustbin of history.

Unfortunately, this couldn't be further from the truth. With his appointment of Suella Braverman – another person of colour – to the role of Home Secretary, we've seen endless dog whistling to pit different races against each other. Following a violent riot outside a hotel in Merseyside containing asylum seekers in which a police van was set alight, Braverman was quick to blame the asylum seekers rather than the far-right groups involved.

Sadly, this was not the first time she'd sought to inflame racial tensions. Braverman has previously complained about the "invasion" of migrants and Nimco Ali, a Government adviser, resigned from her post citing Braverman's "crazy rhetoric", which she argued was helping fuel racism in the UK.

Both Braverman and Sunak appear to be in denial about racism – and Sunak's view that the racism he experienced as a child wouldn't happen today because Britain is a changed country seems at odds with the experiences of many people.

They remind me of the little known women who opposed the rights of other women to vote in the early twentieth century. But equally there is perhaps something more sinister at play here. Another Sunak appointment is the Conservatives deputy chair Lee Anderson (who you'll recall refused to support England because players took the knee). He has argued that the Conservatives need to fight the 2024 election on 'culture wars' and, naturally, migrants will always play a big part in this.

One business leader who quit the Tories after 39-years of membership said, 'It was made pretty clear the plan is to run a culture war to distract from economic failings.'

At a time when Britain's economy is struggling, crime increasing and our NHS overwhelmed, there is a very real likelihood that migrants will once again be sacrificed on the altar of culture wars as part of a plan to stoke divisions.

Fear is all they have left.

This desperately saddens me because weaponising migrants to try and explain away falling living standards is the last desperate throw of the dice from a government that's run out of ideas.

Britain doesn't need a bogeyman in the form of people of colour. It needs a message of hope and a plan to ensure we get the best out of everyone's talent.

We must not fear the opportunity to do better.

FURTHER READING

I drew from a wealth of articles, reports, books, documentaries and journals when researching this book and would like to express my gratitude to all journalists, civil society organisations, think tanks and authors whose work helped me to write it. All the sources cited are freely available online, but in the course of writing this book, I found the following resources to be very useful.

Books and articles
Andrews, Kehinde, 'I compared universities to slave plantations to disturb, not discourage', *The Guardian*, 2016

Bailey, Georgina, 'Ben Wallace interview: UK defence isn't fit for purpose – our armed forces must adapt to 21st century threats', *House Magazine*, 2020

Cameron, David, 'Stand by, universities; I'm bringing the fight for equality in Britain to you', *The Sunday Times*, 2016

Collins, David, '"Killer' of Agnes Wanjiru still at large while army drags feet', *The Sunday Times*, 2022

Cottrell, The Right Rev Stephen, 'Impact of the decline of religion in Britain', *The Times*, 2017

Dey, Monica, 'The Pay and Progression of Women of Colour', *Fawcett Society*, 2021

'Elitist Britain: The educational backgrounds of Britain's leading people', The Sutton Trust, 2019

Engel, Matthew, *Wisden Cricketers' Almanack 1999,* John Wisden, 1999

Francis, Alannah, 'Empowering black people to become academics 'should be top priority' as data reveals poor diversity levels', *The i newspaper*, 2022

Gentleman, Amelia, *The Windrush Betrayal: Exposing the Hostile Environment*, Guardian Faber, 2019

Goldsmith, Zac, 'On Thursday, are we really going to hand the world's greatest city to a Labour Party that thinks terrorists are its friends?', *The Mail on Sunday*, 2016

Green Park Business Leaders Index, Green Park, 2021

Haslam, Alexander & Ryan, Michelle, 'The Glass Cliff: Exploring the dynamics surrounding the appointment off women to precarious leadership positions', *The Academy of Management Review* 2007

Henry, Lenny, 'Regrets, Racism and Me', *The Times*, 2021

'Home Truths: Undoing Racism and delivering real diversity in the charity sector', ACEVO, 2020

Hooks, Bell, *Homegrown: Engaged Cultural Criticism*, Routledge, 2017

John, Professor Gus, 'Independent Comparative Case Review', The Solicitors Regulation Authority, 2014

Kruger, Justin and Dunning, David, 'Unskilled and Unaware of It: how difficulties in recognising one's own incompetence lead to inflated self-assessments', *Journal of Personality and Social Psychology*, 1999

Lammy David, 'The Lammy Review: An Independent Review into the Treatment of, and Outcomes for, Black, Asian and

Minority Ethnic Individuals in the Criminal Justice System', London, 2017

Marble, W, *Can exposure to celebrities reduce prejudice? The Effect of Mohamad Salah on Islamophobic behaviours and attitudes*, Cambridge University Press, 2021

McGregor-Smith, Ruby, 'Race in the workplace: the McGregor-Smith Review', Department for Business, Energy and Industrial Strategy, 2017

McIntosh, Peggy, 'White Privilege: Unpacking the Invisible Knapsack', *Peace and Freedom Magazine*, 1989

Myers, Ella, 'Beyond the Psychological Wage: Du Bois on White Dominion', *Political Theory*, 2018

Nouri, Steve, 'The role of bias in artificial intelligence', *Forbes*, 2021

Oluo, Ijeoma, *Mediocre: The Dangerous Legacy of White Male America*, Seal Press, 2020

Parker, Sir John, 'Ethnic diversity of UK boards: The Parker Review', *Department for Business, Energy and Industrial Strategy*, 2016

Ruzycki, Shannon, Brown, Alison, 'Making medical leadership more diverse', *British Medical Journal*, 2021

Sandel, Michael, *The Tyranny of Merit: What's become of the common good?*, Allen Lane, 2020

Southgate, Gareth, 'Dear England', *The Players' Tribune*, 2021

'State of the nation 2021: social mobility and the pandemic', The Social Mobility Commission, 2021

Syed, Matthew, 'Diversity is not a diversion – it's the West's secret weapon to combat Putin's groupthink', *The Sunday Times*, 2022

'Tackling racial harassment: universities challenged', Equality and Human Rights Commission, 2019

'The Equity Effect', A report from Henley Business School, 2021

Thomas, Cheryl, '2020 UK Judicial Attitudes Survey', UCL Judicial Institute, 2021

Townley, Lynne, Kaul, Kaly, 'In the Age of 'Us Too?': Moving Towards A Zero-Tolerance Attitude To Harassment and Bullying at the Bar - A Report on the Association of Women Barristers' Roundtable on harassment and Bullying With Recommendations', *City Law School Research Paper No. 2019/07*, 2019

Tyler, Richard, 'What I learnt…about hiring bias', *The Times*, 2022

Wilson, Fraser, 'Former Celtic Boss John Barnes makes impassioned plea as he calls for bigots to 'own up' to their black manager bias', *Daily Record*, 2020

TV & Video

Adey, Linda, *Is Uni Racist?* BBC Three, 2021 https://www.bbc.co .uk/programmes/p09dhr3f

Myrie, Clive, *Is the Church Racist?* BBC Panorama, 2021

Rafiq, Azeem, *DCMS Hearing* https://www.youtube.com/watch? v=Dj2WrXy60pc, 2021

ACKNOWLEDGEMENTS

First I want to thank those who contributed, both on and off the record, without whom I would have nothing to share. I want to acknowledge the immense contribution of my collaborator, Matt Baker, without whom it might have been a couple more years before you were able to read this.

Then there was the support of a diverse group of experts, including (though not exclusively) Professor Barnie Choudhury, Dr Bela Arora, Dr Roxanne Khan, Lynne Townley, Ilina Trendafilova, Carol Ann Whitehead, Sadia Humayun and my colleagues at Hopwood Hall College.

Of course, the book in your hand would not exist without my publishers, Jonathan de Peyer and the great people at HarperNorth.

Finally, my hope for the future came from my children, Marina, Shaan, Samir and Kabir, whose wisdom belies their years.

Thank you all.

Nazir Afzal, OBE
July 2022

Harper North

would like to thank the following staff and contributors for their
involvement in making this book a reality:

Hannah Avery

Fionnuala Barrett

Claire Boal

Charlotte Brown

Sarah Burke

Alan Cracknell

Aya Daghem

Jonathan de Peyer

Anna Derkacz

Tom Dunstan

Kate Elton

Rachel Evans

Mick Fawcett

Simon Gerratt

Monica Green

Natassa Hadjinicolaou

Lauren Harris

Ben Hurd

Megan Jones

Mike Jones

Jean-Marie Kelly

Oliver Malcolm

Alice Murphy-Pyle

Adam Murray

Genevieve Pegg

Agnes Rigou

James Ryan

Florence Shepherd

Eleanor Slater

Emma Sullivan

Katrina Troy

Phillipa Walker

Kelly Webster